"Morally unflinching, intellectually courageous, Rabbi John Rosove has provided us with a desperately needed map for how to navigate the growing tensions between progressives and the state of Israel. By calling out Israel when it has done wrong and calling out its critics when they exaggerate Israel's flaws, Rabbi Rosove echoes the ancient prophets, who criticized their people but always loved and defended them. This thoughtful and passionate book reminds us that commitment to Israel and to social justice are essential components of a healthy Jewish identity."
—**Yossi Klein Halevi,**
    Senior Fellow, Shalom Hartman Institute, Jerusalem

"Rabbi John Rosove's letters to his sons, published in this volume, are tender and loving, but also gripping and challenging, as he grapples with modern Israel, Jewish identity, relations between Israelis and Diaspora Jews, and perhaps most significantly whether 'you can maintain your ethical and moral values while at the same time being supporters of the Jewish state despite its flaws and imperfections.'
"Rosove pulls no punches, laying out both the imperfections and the ethical choices surrounding Israel and American Jews. But he also manifests a passionate love for Israel and what one scholar has called 'values-based aspirational Zionism.' This book will raise as many questions for Rosove's sons as it answers; it is a book that many of us wish we had written for our own children."
—**Daniel Kurtzer,**
    S. Daniel Abraham Professor in Middle Eastern Policy Studies, Princeton University's Woodrow Wilson School of Public and International Affairs;
    Former U.S. Ambassador to Israel (2001-2005) and U.S. Ambassador to Egypt (1997-2001)

"A moving love letter to Israel from a rabbinic leader who refuses to give into despair, but instead recommits to building a democratic Israel that lives up to the vision of its founders."
—**Rabbi Jill Jacobs,**
    Executive Director, T'ruah: The Rabbinic Call for Human Rights

"What a marvelous and refreshing book! A liberal social activist and committed Reform Jew, Rosove makes the case to Jewish millennials that they need Israel as a source of pride, connection, and Jewish renewal, and Israel needs them for the liberal values that they can bring to the Zionist enterprise. In its call for 'aspirational Zionism,' the book is honest and tough about Israel's flaws, but optimistic about the country's direction and filled with practical strategies for promoting change. This is a no-nonsense, straight-talking work, intellectually rigorous but deeply personal. And most important, it demonstrates in compelling prose to young Jews—and Jews of all ages—that Jewish life cannot be sustained without Israel at its core."
—**Rabbi Eric H. Yoffie,**
President Emeritus, Union for Reform Judaism

"In a beautifully written, passionate, emotional and heartfelt book, Rabbi Rosove describes his love for Israel. Always honest, authentic and sincere, John does not attempt to hide Israel's imperfections. His forty years in the rabbinate taught him that anything human is imperfect, and that true love requires engagement in the work of improvement and repair.

"The form of Rabbi Rosove's book is a series of touching letters to his adult children. In this way, John writes to all our children. Read and reread Rabbi Rosove's book. Turn the pages over and over again. You will glean his spirit, and the spirit of our people that has created and sustained the State of Israel—one of the great miracles of the world."
—**Rabbi Ammiel Hirsch,**
Senior Rabbi, Stephen Wise Free Synagogue, New York City

"Through a series of letters to his sons, Rabbi John Rosove movingly describes his own relationship to the State of Israel and provides advice and a way forward for a new generation to forge its own relationship with the Jewish State. Rosove's optimism, and his boundless faith in Jewish peoplehood and Jewish values, makes this book an invaluable blueprint for Jews, both in Israel and around the world, to help the Jewish State live up to its founding values of acceptance, pluralism, and democracy and become a true light unto the nations."
—**Anat Hoffman,**
Executive Director, Israel Religious Action Center

"As in his previous book—*Why Judaism Matters, Letters of a Liberal Rabbi to His Children and the Millennial Generation*—in *Why Israel and Its Future Matter, Letters of a Liberal Rabbi to His Children and the Millennial Generation*, Rabbi John L. Rosove shares 11 compelling letters directed at his two sons, but this fascinating work is in fact aimed at an entire generation of perplexed young Jews.

"Diaspora Jewry is in a struggle for its collective identity and the Millennial generation all the more so. In an era of FAKE, truth becomes a spiritual commodity; a period of ANTI and POST demands value- based motivation, sound reasoning, active listening, and candid conversation. This is what Rabbi Rosove provides this readership. He delineates the just case for Israel with precision and delicacy, sans fluff or pandering. This is a book which strives to combat Israel haters and bashers and gives real tools and answers to those liberal Jews who feel somewhat frustrated and confused about Israel.

"Rabbi Rosove's truths reach minds and open hearts. I urge each and every individual who feels in any way connected to the Jewish People, to ponder this powerful assemblage of candid, insightful messages which address the core issues facing Israel as a nation, and as a notion.

A must-read!"
   —Isaac Herzog
      Chairman, Jewish Agency for Israel

"At a moment of looming crisis, when young Jews in America are increasingly alienated from Israel, Rabbi John Rosove offers this timely, wise, and candid reflection on the fate of Zionism in the twenty-first century. In the form of letters to his sons, he formulates compelling answers to one of the most difficult questions of our time: why should we care? More particularly, why should young Jews care about an Israel that does not reflect their political and moral sensibilities? His missives are essential reading for all concerned with the Jewish condition today."
   —David N. Myers,
      Kahn Professor of Jewish History, UCLA;
      President of the Board, New Israel Fund

"As the distance grows between many Diaspora Jews with Israel, Rabbi John Rosove offers key insights to the critical question of why Israel matters and should be a part of our lives as Jews. His lifelong commitment to a Jewish and democratic State of Israel, to the growth of the Reform Movement, and for social justice in Israel has manifested throughout his illustrious career as rabbi and Jewish leader and features prominently in this important contribution to the Jewish bookshelf.

"Each of the 11 letters offers a unique and digestible approach to a topic of significance to this broad discussion. Rabbi Rosove's frank style and deliberate directness allow readers to come away with clear understandings of complex concepts and easily adopt them to their own understanding and to that of others.

"The book is a must-read for countless Diaspora Jews looking for information and different ways to comprehend the significance of modern-day Israel. Rabbi Rosove offers not only for his sons, but for educators looking for new material, guiding questions, and matter of fact explanations.

"With everything he offers us in this short volume Rabbi Rosove teaches us to never give up hope, which makes this a must-read for all."
—**Rabbi Josh Weinberg**
    VP for Israel and Reform Zionism, Union for Reform Judaism;
    Director, Association of Reform Zionists of America

"Rabbi Rosove's voice is an important, timely addition to the conversation on the American Jewish community's relationship to Israel and Palestine. Through the lens of a father's hopes and concerns for his sons, he challenges us to approach this conflict with the same generosity and compassion as he does. A must-read for those inside the community and out who are not just looking for the right answers, but the right questions."
—**Brooke Davies,**
    Former President of the J Street U National Board

Why Israel (and its Future) Matters

Letters of a Liberal Rabbi To His Children and the Millennial Generation

RABBI JOHN L. ROSOVE

בכבוד

John L Rosove 1/19/20

Ben Yehuda Press

Teaneck, New Jersey

Published by Ben Yehuda Press
122 Ayers Court Suite 1B
Teaneck, NJ 07666

http://www.BenYehudaPress.com

To subscribe to our monthly book club and support independent Jewish publishing, visit https://www.patreon.com/BenYehudaPress

ISBN13 978-1-934730-83-6

Library of Congress Cataloging-in-Publication Data

Names: Rosove, John L., author.
Title: Why Israel (and its future) matters : letters of a liberal rabbi to
  his children and the millennial generation / John L. Rosove.
Description: Teaneck, NJ : Ben Yehuda Press, 2019. | Includes
  bibliographical references. | Summary: "Presented in the form of letters
  from a rabbi to his sons, Why Israel (and its Future) Matters) makes the

  case to Jewish millennials that they need Israel as a source of pride,
  connection, and Jewish renewal, and Israel needs them for the liberal
  values that they can bring to the Zionist enterprise"-- Provided by
  publisher.
Identifiers: LCCN 2019030616 | ISBN 9781934730836 (trade paperback)
Subjects: LCSH: Jews--United States--Attitudes toward Israel. |
  Zionism--United States. | Reform Zionism--United States. | Jews--United
  States--Identity.
Classification: LCC DS132 .R67 2019 | DDC 320.54095694--dc23
LC record available at https://lccn.loc.gov/2019030616

19 20 21 / 10 9 8 7 6 5 4 3 2 1   20191031

For Daniel, Marina, and David

In gratitude to Barbara

In Memory
of all who sacrificed their lives
and built the State of Israel

Contents

Preface

I chose to write a series of letters to my own millennial children and, by extension, to all our millennial children as a vehicle to speak personally to their questions, doubts, struggles, and need to understand why our relationship with the State of Israel matters for our own future and the future of the people of Israel.

I seek in these letters to probe the thinking of young American Jews (and their parents) that transcends the day-to-day disturbing headlines and beyond the polarization that has widened between many Israelis and liberal American Jews in recent years and between liberal and conservative American Jews when discussing Israel, its policies and its aspirations.

By breaking down the many questions and issues into thematic units and then following up with questions at the end of each letter, I hope to stimulate conversation and dialogue between parents and their grown children as well as in synagogue communities, chavurot, teen programming, Hillel chapters, and university classes to think about American liberal Jewish identity in relationship to the State of Israel.

I also hope that these letters may provoke conversation between American liberal Jews and Israelis about our relationship with each other to find common ground.

Introduction:
An Invitation to a Tough,
Important Conversation

Dear Daniel and David,

As your father I've always asked you to think for yourselves as independent, responsible and kind-hearted human beings. Those are essential Jewish values and virtues. Mom and I have sought to apply them to every relationship we have—at home, among friends, in the workplace, with strangers, and with those with whom we disagree. We've also shown you a way to regard our religious tradition as a means for connecting with the eternal in ourselves and in others, and as a source of great wisdom for navigating the dilemmas of being human in our often perplexing world. And we've raised you to identify strongly as Jews. I've tried to show you, by example, thought, and deed, the depth of my commitment to the Jewish people and the State of Israel.

I want to start this series of letters about why I believe that Israel matters so much to us and to the Jewish people by telling you about one of the most inspiring and uplifting moments in my young adult life as a Jew. I get chills even now whenever I think of it.

I was studying Hebrew at Ulpan Akiva (an accelerated Hebrew language immersion course) in Netanya for two months during the summer of 1973 before I began my first year of rabbinic studies in Jerusalem. With me at the ulpan were Jews who had recently made aliyah to Israel from around the world, plus a few East Jerusalem and West Bank Arabs. We studied in an enriched Hebrew language environment just walking distance from the Mediterranean shore.

The ulpan planned regular excursion tours for its students. Among the most powerful of those tours for me was traveling to Tel Aviv to attend the opening ceremonies of the Maccabean Games—the Jewish Olympics held every four years in Israel, drawing Jewish athletes from around the world. We got to see each country's team march into the stadium.

After the last team entered, a lone runner carrying a torch circled the track, turned through a gate into the stands, and climbed the stairs to the top; there, a huge 11-branched menorah was waiting to be kindled in memory of the 11 Israeli Olympic athletes murdered by the Palestinian Black September terrorist organization at the 1972 Munich Olympic Games.

As he began to light the flames, we 45,000 rose to our feet and fell silent, and when he kindled the eleventh candle we sang Hatikvah ("The Hope"), Israel's national anthem. That full and overwhelming chorus of voices singing that moving melody has never left me. I get chills up and down my body thinking how I felt then, and each time I sing Hatikvah I'm transported back to that Tel Aviv stadium amidst 45,000 of our people.

Another memorable and transformative Jewish memory: On the afternoon of Yom Kippur, October 6, 1973, minutes before 2:00 p.m., I was sitting on my dorm balcony in the Rehavia neighborhood of Jerusalem when air-raid sirens sounded throughout Jerusalem and the State of Israel. I turned on the radio to the BBC channel and I learned that 1,300 Syrian tanks had just crossed the border into Israel in the north and that the Egyptian army had attacked Israel from across the Bar Lev Line in the south, signaling that Israel was at war for the third time in its 25-year history.

The Yom Kippur War (as it came to be called), launched on the Jewish people's holiest day, was among the most traumatic wars in the history of the state. Though Israel was ultimately victorious on the battlefield after 20 days of fighting, victory wasn't a given. On the tenth day of the war, then Prime Minister Golda Meir urgently called the Israeli Ambassador to the United States in Washington, D.C., Simcha Dinitz, to tell him that all of Israel's armaments and ammunition were at the front and that the Jewish state needed an immediate and massive airlift of arms from the United States to survive. President Richard Nixon responded; Israel's stockpile was replenished and the Jewish state went on to win the war on the battlefield.

During those three weeks I worked nights as a volunteer at one of the large bakeries in Jerusalem—the Berman Bakery—taking the place of young Israelis who had been called to their units. Each night around 9:00 p.m. I was picked up from a central location and taken to the bakery, and before dawn I was returned to that point. From there, through darkened streets, I walked the mile to my dorm.

Jerusalem was under order for a complete blackout so enemy pilots couldn't see well enough to bomb Jewish neighborhoods. The quiet of the Jerusalem night under a blanket of stars was eerily beautiful. I remember thinking for the first time in my life that from the center of the Jewish world in the holiest city in Judaism, I was a participant in Jewish history.

Some 30 years later I had lunch with my friend Yossi Klein Halevi in the Emek Refaim neighborhood of Jerusalem. Yossi is a significant Jewish thought leader today, a writer and scholar at the Shalom Hartman Institute in Jerusalem. He was born in New York, the child of Holocaust survivors, and came on aliyah to Israel in the early 1980s.

I asked Yossi why he came to Israel on aliyah. He said: "As a Jew and a journalist, I wanted to write from the center of Jewish history, not the periphery—and the center of Jewish history and the Jewish world is here in Israel."

I had heard this message many years earlier from Rabbi Richard Hirsch, the founding Director of the Religious Action Center of Reform Judaism in Washington, D.C., who made aliyah with his family in 1972. A Zionist from his youth, Dick had come to the conclusion that if the Reform movement was ever to have historic significance, it had to have a center in the State of Israel. He was also serving at the time as the President of the World Union for Progressive Judaism (WUPJ), the international Reform movement, and as he made aliyah he moved the WUPJ center from New York to Jerusalem.

Dick had famously told the Board of Trustees of the Reform movement—to the consternation of many powerful American Jewish leaders who were not Zionists and who criticized him heavily for making this statement—"Israel is Broadway; America is off-Broadway!"

I agree with Dick. As you know, Israel flows through my veins. Our family members were early pioneers arriving in Jaffa in 1880. They lived in Jerusalem for two years until, with three other families, they established the first Jewish village of Petach Tikvah outside the Old City of Jerusalem in 1882.

During my year of study in Jerusalem (1973-1974), I spent many Shabbatot with our cousins there and I seriously considered making aliyah, but my rabbinic studies in the United States and our family kept me here in America. Despite living my life outside of Israel, I resonate with the words of the eleventh century physician, poet and philosopher Yehuda Halevi who said *"Libi b'mizrach, v'anochi b'kitz'rei ma'arav*—My heart is in the east, and the rest of me is at the extremities of the west."

I share this with you to express how deeply Zionism and the State of Israel live in my heart and are at the core of my identity as a Jew. I don't expect you necessarily to feel the same way I do, but I hope that you will appreciate how central the land, people and State of Israel are not only to me, but to the Jewish people in Israel and the Jewish Diaspora—and become leaders in your generation on behalf of Israel and progressive (i.e., liberal) Zionism.

In these letters I will tell you why Israel is so important to me, why I believe that Israel holds such promise for our people and all peoples, what I'm most worried about concerning the Israel of today, and how you and your generation of millennial American Jews ought to relate to Zionism and the Jewish state.

Love,

Dad

Discussion questions:

- Have you visited Israel and what was your experience there? Positive or negative?

- What were some of the most meaningful moments for you in Israel?

- The author discusses his experiences in Israel before, during and after the 1973 Yom Kippur War. What has been your own emotional reaction when Israel has been the target of terrorist attack or been fighting a war?

- Could you ever see yourself making aliyah and if so what would be your motivation? If not, why not?

Our American Jewish Identity and Israel— Finding Common Ground

Dear Daniel and David,

I pinch myself that we have lived our entire lives with a Jewish State of Israel. It had not been so for Jews for 2,000 years. Our ancestors prayed toward Jerusalem and affirmed at the end of every Passover Seder— "*Bashanah ha-ba-ah biY'ru-sha-la-yim*/Next year in Jerusalem"—but they had no way of going there before the end of the nineteenth century when the Zionist movement began.

The fact of Israel's existence as a sovereign nation today is not only an event of historic proportions, but it ushers in an entirely new set of practical burdens and moral responsibilities—the principle one of which is how to rule ethically while wielding political and military power.

We liberal American Jews have had a very different experience and we've lived in a very different environment than have our Israeli brothers and sisters. Here in America we are a small minority population comprising about 1.6 percent of the United States. Though we American Jews have risen to positions of influence and power at the highest levels of government, diplomacy, politics, business, labor, the professions, and the arts, we American Jews do not have the responsibility to protect and secure a people and nation as do the leaders of the Jewish state.

Here in the United States we Jews have had the task primarily to build our communities and raise our families, based upon core American principles of inclusiveness and respect for the other. Here we've been called to see our own face in the face of the stranger, to honor the rights of others, to value social justice and compassion. Our sometimes-tortured Jewish history has left us with an indelible sense of what it is to be stripped of basic human worth and human rights. Consequently, we American Jews respond powerfully to the toxic and destructive effects of violence and injustice, and we're drawn to side with the oppressed.

That's why the subject of Zionism and the State of Israel is so fraught for so many Jews, and it's one of the reasons I'm writing these letters to you: to show you a path on which you can maintain your ethical and moral values while at the same time being supporters of the Jewish state, despite its flaws and imperfections.

Here in the United States there seems to be a simple, clean, values-driven line that we liberal Jews have drawn in most situations: side with the oppressed, not the oppressor. Israel is a vital parliamentary democracy within the Green Line—the 1949 armistice lines that separate Israel from the West Bank—in which the majority population is Jewish. Life on the other side of the Green Line and in East Jerusalem—where the majority population is Arab but controlled by Israel—is rife with injustice, inequality and oppression. The Palestinian Arabs living in the West Bank are controlled by a military administration that has raised moral and ethical challenges to foundational Israeli values as enshrined in its Declaration of Independence, and to our own liberal American Jewish values.

In this context many have wondered whether Israel has become an oppressor. Has Israel sacrificed our liberal Jewish values that emphasize compassion and justice? Is that what I'm asking you to do when I ask you to identify with and support the Jewish State?

We also have to evaluate our support for the State of Israel in the context of disturbing trends in the United States and across the world. In stunning ways since the election of Donald Trump we've been challenged by a nationalist/nativist surge that threatens traditions of democracy here and in many places in the world. Contrary to both the American and Jewish ethic, the President has demonized the outsider and closed American borders to suffering refugees fleeing for their lives and the lives of their children. Here in America many of our current policies are morally toxic and contrary to our democratic and Jewish traditions.

When thinking of the Israeli occupation of the West Bank, many liberal American Jews have asked themselves: Why not boycott and divest from and sanction Israel if it's engaging in similarly toxic behavior? Why not just focus on building our own families and an American community while fighting for more enlightened Jewish ideals in this country, and wash our hands of the Jewish state and let Israelis fend for themselves?

These are hard questions. But despite the imperfections and moral challenges that Israel faces, I hold fast to the position that it's vital for you to continue to believe in Israel. Understand and see its promise. Accept it with its flaws while remaining impatient for justice. Help those of like mind in Israel (and there are hundreds of thousands of Israelis who believe as we liberal American Jews believe) to find its way to being what the State of Israel was always meant to be and in many ways already is—"a light to the nations" (Isaiah 49:6).

This means not only understanding Israel's history, but considering your own identity as a Jew and what Israel means to you. For you and others of your generation, no matter how distant or skeptical you feel about what you hear, remember this: Israel is singularly the greatest accomplishment of the Jewish people in 2,000 years. It's also a mirror of our people. It's a connection to our spiritual DNA. Most importantly, it's a vision of the future that's deeply Jewish and deeply human.

What I believe is true in this tumultuous and critical time in world history is this: the most important battles are and will be fought over values. That's what is playing out in Israel. In its Declaration of Independence, the founders' aspirations are clear and described this way:

> [The State of Israel] will foster the development of the country for the benefit of all its inhabitants; it will be based on freedom, justice and peace as envisaged by the prophets of Israel; it will ensure complete equality of social and political rights to all its inhabitants irrespective of religion, race or sex; it will guarantee freedom of religion, conscience, language, education and culture; it will safeguard the Holy Places of all religions; and it will be faithful to the principles of the Charter of the United Nations.

The Biblical prophets guided us for three millennia with words such as, "Show mercy and compassion, each person to another; and do not oppress the widow or the fatherless, the stranger or the poor…" (Zechariah 7:9-10). More importantly, they instructed us to spread a vision of peace in the world through the example of Israel. The prophets were visionaries and realists. They understood the human condition with all its dark corners, even as they sought to lift the nation to a higher plane in which justice, compassion and peace were defining values. That's our millennia-old Jewish legacy, as Isaiah admonished: "And they shall beat their swords into plowshares and their spears into pruning-hooks; nation shall not lift up sword against nation, neither shall they learn war anymore" (Isaiah 2:4).

The distance between here and there—the Israel that is and that ought to be and the America that is and ought to be—is vast, and you and your generation will be the ones to carry that vision into the future. Because you've been raised with liberal Jewish values to be compassionate and just human beings, I hope that you'll also stay tied to the people, land and State of Israel. You are the ones who will be called upon to help protect them, advocate for them, join with Israelis who feel and believe as you do—who want social justice and yearn for peace—and who need your support to amplify their voices and values as Israel moves forward as a nation.

I know you'll use tools my generation never had to bridge gaps, reach across divides and find common ground with those—Arab, Israeli, American, orthodox, liberal, Jew, Christian, and Muslim—who seek this just, egalitarian peace.

For our family, part of which fled anti-Semitic oppression in Lithuania in 1880 and arrived in Palestine with the first wave of Jewish immigrants, Palestine was a refuge. My great-great Uncle Avraham Shapira, who died before you were born but not before I met him, was the first policeman in the first Jewish settlement outside of Jerusalem at Petach Tikvah, and acted as guide and bodyguard for Theodor Herzl, the father of Zionism, and Chaim Weizmann, Israel's first President, whenever they visited Palestine.

In Weizmann's autobiography, he describes my great-great uncle in a way that evokes much of which we face today:

> Abraham Shapira was in himself a symbol of a whole process of Jewish re-adaptation. He accompanied me on most of my trips up and down Palestine, partly as guide, partly as guard, and all the while I listened to his epic stories of the

old-time colonists. He was a primitive person, spoke better Arabic than Hebrew, and seemed so much a part of the rocks and stony hillsides of the country that it was difficult to believe that he had been born in Lithuania. Here was a man who in his own lifetime had bridged a gap of thousands of years; who, once in Palestine, had shed his Galut [i.e. Diaspora] environment like an old coat...[1]

Our family members were newcomers hungry for safety, people whose survival hinged on learning the land and the language of their new Arab neighbors—as well as mastering the Hebrew that would bind them and us together with those from every corner of the Diaspora. As our people built the infrastructure of a future Jewish state in the initial decades of the twentieth century, Jews clung to this place—especially after the trauma of the Holocaust. They equated Israel with a phoenix rising from the ashes and bringing our people back into history from near annihilation. Safety and security were and continue to be everything to us.

Two generations removed from the trauma, though—and, thankfully, with a far less visceral, defining sense of fear—your sense of Israel, as you witness it from America, is understandably different than mine; perhaps less forgiving and more frustrating, though I confess that I often share your frustration. There's less urgency for you to parse the twists of history that brought us to this vexing moment, more of a tendency to throw up your hands and turn away as too many millennial Jews are now doing, if polls are accurate.[2]

To support an aspirational, justice-based vision of Israel's future, you need to know the historic terrain, the dual narratives of Israeli Jew and Palestinian Arab, and the ways in which a Wikipedia entry on the history of Israel can lead you toward an unhelpful and un-nuanced understanding of how today's situation evolved. Without letting the conversation devolve into an alphabet soup of acronyms of Jewish and Zionist organizations and an impenetrable thicket of history, I'll offer you a streamlined look at the shifting imperatives and alliances that have shaped the country's history and color today's possibilities. You can find the most important highlights of Zionist and Israeli history in the Appendix. Do take a look at it.

Through these letters, I hope to share my passion and love for Israel and why I care so much about her well-being. I also want to encourage you and your peers to embrace the deep and enduring idea of Israel and bring your minds, hearts, vision, and boundless talent to help that ancient land, modern state, and our people there to finally embody peace.

I hope these letters will inform and inspire you, touch and enlighten you about the remarkable nation that our people has built since Theodor Herzl first convened the World Zionist Congress in 1897 in Brussels, Belgium. Israel is a miracle of Jewish history and it belongs to us and every Jew, even though we live outside the land.

Love,

Dad

Discussion Questions

- How do you believe that the experience of the Diaspora Jewish community has changed since the establishment of the State of Israel?

- As you listen to and read the news about Israel, have you at any time felt that your liberal Jewish values are in conflict with the choices that the government and military of Israel have taken? If so, what specific actions have challenged you and your values?

- The author cites his great-great uncle Avraham Shapira and quotes from Chaim Weizmann's autobiography describing how Shapira was a "symbol of a whole process of Jewish re-adaptation." Given that we live in a different era of Jewish history, how might you need to change the way you think about Israel in order to accept the challenges Israel faces today?

Israel and the Idea of Home

Dear Daniel and David,

In thinking about our relationship to Israel, there's an undercurrent that colors almost everything. It has to do with our sense of home as individuals and as Jews, and also with our sense of belonging to a place and what creates that sense of belonging for us in the world. So in considering the idea of liberal and progressive Zionism and why I believe you can and should support it, I'd like to start in that very personal realm of belonging to a place and the meaning of home.

What's home to you?

In the simplest sense, it might be the house you grew up in, the house where your mom and I still live. It's a place filled with memory, acceptance, and evidence of who you've been and would become. As the familiar Robert Frost lines put it, it will always be the place "where when you have to go there, they have to take you in." It's also, as Frost added, a place you don't have to earn, a place you "somehow haven't to deserve."

That home is nested within the home our family has made in the United States. We share the language, culture, history, aspirations, and ideals that define America to itself, and we have the American sense that those commonalities bind us together with our neighbors to create a shared vision of our country, a unified whole. We see the challenges to that common vision every day, yet we hold to the idea that our Americanness can be bigger than our differences. America is where we're from, and Americans are who we are.

At the same time, we're also Jews. And that gives us a more nuanced sense of what it means to belong in the place we've chosen to live.

The old myth of America was that all of us would (could) drop our given identities—religious, tribal, ethnic, racial, national, political, economic, cultural and every other—into the melting pot and, in a few generations, refashion ourselves into self-defined Americans, individuals not bound by the class or background we came from. Our sense of belonging here would come from declaring it, choosing our own "tribes," freely shaping our own identities and joining with similarly free people unified by the belief that all of us have the opportunity to prosper and feel America's embrace—if only we work hard enough.

We've seen how that's turned out. Success for some came amidst a long history of bias and aggression aimed at a gallery of those labeled *other* and kept on the margins. Up until the Second World War, anti-Semitism permeated much of America and no matter what my parents and grandparents did, they could only assimilate so much.

In today's America, the ground seems suddenly to be shifting quickly beneath our feet, particularly since the ascendency of Trump to the presidency with his inflammatory rhetoric and legendary insensitivity toward minorities, as Muslims, Jews, young black men, Mexican and Latino immigrant families, the LGBTQ community, and kids who resist gun violence—to name just a few—all find themselves as targets of political and social attack. The rhetoric facing these groups as they find themselves singled out is dehumanizing and, quite frankly, disgusting; and as it echoes through the culture, the violence and intolerance directed at them increase too.

We see evidence daily that democracy, acceptance and equality are fragile—just as are our democratic institutions that have been under attack since the 2016 presidential election. Without constant care, the social fabric rips. The ideal of inclusion vaporizes, leaving fear, discrimination, and hate in its place.

I've been thinking about all this a lot lately because of a recent worrisome study of Jews in the San Francisco Bay area that reported that many in your generation are only loosely tethered to a sense of Jewish identity and connection to Israel. You are "more spiritual and less ethnic, and Israel falls in the ethnic compartment," reported the people interpreting the study. They also described you and your peers (at least in very liberal northern California) as more universalistic in your outlook and less attached to the Jewish people or tribe.[1] If that's true, I think that many in your generation are aligned with that classic American sense that we can cast our inherited identity into the melting pot and embrace self-definition without the constraints that come with a specific cultural and ethnic heritage.

Though there's a sense of liberation that comes with doing that, there's also a caveat, which became abundantly clear to many Millennials with the rise of the alt-right and Trump-backing white supremacists and nationalists in the presidential campaign of 2016: No matter how you identify yourself, your background/tribe/ethnicity—that is, your Jewishness—is inescapable. History, as we know too well, has often made Jews the demonized *other*.

Many of your peers were smacked with the reality personally for the first time when the President retweeted the Pepe the Frog meme and tacitly endorsed swastika-covered hate. For others the jolt came when so many politicians refused to denounce David Duke of the Ku Klux Klan as he ran for president, governor and Senate in Louisiana in the 1990s.

Politico surveyed the shock in the Jewish Millennial community, quoting one activist as saying, "For a long time we were told that anti-Semitism was everywhere, and we rolled our eyes at that. This feels like the closest thing to the type of anti-Semitism that my grandparents talk about experiencing in Poland."[2]

We thought we were beyond that kind of blatant hatred in America, and then there it was, as clear as day.

All of us, across the generations, were stunned in the summer of 2017 when white supremacists carrying Nazi flags and wearing T-shirts quoting Hitler marched in Charlottesville, Virginia. I can't erase from my mind the image of Nazis with semi-automatic machine guns standing across the street from Congregation Beth Israel, a Reform synagogue in the city, as worshippers attended Shabbat services. The supremacists' desire to intimidate was unmistakable. Almost worse, the local police refused to protect those Jewish citizens. For the first time, the synagogue hired a private security firm to ensure the safety of its congregants as they were coming and going from Shabbat services.

Even the most assimilated and "least Jewish" among us were chilled. We now knew the guns were aimed at us.

In downtown Charlottesville that day, neo-Nazis yelled "blood and soil" (the same words the German Nazis of the 1930s shouted in their marches), "The Jews will not replace us," and a white supremacist murdered a protestor by deliberately ramming his car into a crowd protesting President Trump's nativism and bigotry. The next day, the President condemned the violence but shocked the nation when he called many of the Nazi demonstrators "good people," thereby morally equating them with those who came to protest their hatred and bigotry.

We American Jews still somehow thought we were safe from violence. But then an openly anti-Semitic white nationalist murdered 11 Jews on Shabbat morning, October 27, 2018 at the Tree of Life Synagogue in Pittsburgh. It was the most violent attack on the Jewish community in American history. We know now, if we didn't before, that the Jewish people remain eternal scapegoats for haters and that hatred can turn to violence quickly. What was shocking for some is that old world anti-Semitism has now come to America.

So many of us wonder what has happened to our country. I often think about what it must have been like for Jews living in Germany in the 1930s. I've spoken with German refugees and Holocaust survivors about their experiences then. I've read histories of the period and I've visited the Holocaust museums in Los Angeles, Washington, D.C., and Jerusalem. I've seen the documentaries and listened to survivors' testimony as recorded by the Shoah Foundation.

Let me be clear: Charlottesville and Pittsburgh are very far from 1930s Berlin, yet the events there made me feel vulnerable as a Jew in a way I've never experienced before in America, my home. The rise of nativist-nationalism in the United States, a frightening rise of the same in Europe, and a burst of anti-Semitism in Putin's Russia have given me pause and remind me that what happened in Germany can happen here if good people aren't vigilant in protecting and preserving American democratic institutions. I've thought that despite America being our "home" we ought not to assume that it's a foregone conclusion that being Jewish in America is always going to be safe for us.

I'm shining a light on these events, but I don't want to overstate the threat. Although anti-Semitic incidents have increased dramatically since Trump became President—1,986 in 2017, the Anti-Defamation League reported, the second highest number in 40 years—anti-Semitism is still not part of any organized political movement of note in America today and I don't believe it's any longer part of the fabric of American society.[3]

However, I don't think we can soft-pedal the reality. What happened in Charlottesville and Pittsburgh brought to the surface the sense of precariousness that we Jews have always felt in adopted homes that seem to embrace us. Integrated and assimilated as we are, we're also the *other*.

How Israel Changed Everything

I'd like to make the case that one reason we can regard Charlottesville and Pittsburgh with great concern, but without the existential fear that clung to us in the past, is that the existence of Israel has significantly changed the world and our place in it. Imperfect as it is, and as much as it needs to grow past what it is today, the Jewish state has given us Jews sovereignty. Israel has brought together Jews from around the world to create a nation where, unified by a common history, language (Hebrew), culture, values, and narrative, we're free to embrace our Jewish identity without apology, without questioning our worth as human beings, without demands for loyalty that involve giving up who we are. We as Jews have dominion over ourselves. That's the core idea embedded in the State of Israel. It can embody for us a deeply rooted sense of safety, belonging, self-determination, and home.

That sense is visceral to me, as it may not yet be to you, because my generation and your grandparents' generation witnessed tremendous extremes in Jewish history, and we have experienced the way our fortunes in America changed as Israel was founded, got to its feet and gained strength.

My mother told me stories about being beaten up as a child by school bullies because she was Jewish. Those years of her youth in the 1920s and 1930s were fraught with the anti-Semitism of Father Charles Coughlin, a Roman Catholic priest who used the radio to broadcast nationally his anti-Semitic sermons.

Anti-Semitism reached into the upper echelons of society in those days. Henry Ford was an anti-Semite who published the newspaper *The Dearborn Independent*, also known as *The Ford International Weekly*—and in its pages spewed his hatred of Jews. Charles Lindbergh, the greatest American hero of the 1930s, was unabashedly pro-Nazi and anti-Semitic.

Though President Harry Truman's best friend Eddie Jacobson was a Jew and persuaded Truman to endorse the establishment of the State of Israel minutes after it was declared, Truman, too, held onto anti-Semitic stereotypes.

Before Israel was established, being an American Jew meant trying to keep a low profile and avoid conflict, working to belong while knowing you'd be excluded from many universities, businesses, professions, neighborhoods, hotels, and private clubs—a wide swath of American life.

After Israel came into being in 1948, however, there was a sea change in American Jewish identity and in how Americans felt about and regarded Jews. We traded our victim and outsider status for the dignity that comes with national self-determination.

Two Seminal Childhood Memories

My earliest understanding of what it means to be Jewish was bookended by those two poles of our people's experience. When I was about five years old I found in my father's study a copy of *Life Magazine* that showed photographs of the Nazi concentration camps after their liberation by American soldiers at the end of World War II. My dad probably should not have had that magazine anywhere I could find it; the photographs of emaciated survivors and piles of bodies terrified and confused me at far too young an age and burned the memory of those pictures into my mind, heart, and soul.

I was around the same age in 1956 when I met my great-great Uncle Avraham Shapira at my aunt's and uncle's house in Los Angeles. My parents told me that Uncle Avram, who was then 86 years old, was an important Israeli leader and pioneer. I remember him as strong, powerful, resolute, sure, and independent. To me, he personified the State of Israel—a force to be reckoned with, a protector, and the answer to those horrific photos.

Frankly, Uncle Avram frightened me. He was a very large man and I remember his image to this day. Years later I read Leon Uris' 1958 historical novel *The Exodus* (made in 1960 into an Academy Award-nominated motion picture starring Paul Newman and Eva Marie Saint). When I spent my first year in rabbinic school around the time of the Yom Kippur War in 1973, Uncle Avram's niece and nephew in Petach Tikva told me about incidents in Uncle Avram's life. Many of those incidents were portrayed in the novel's character Barak, played by Paul Newman in the movie.

My cousins told me that one night in the early years in Petach Tikva, thieves from a surrounding Arab village came at night and stole Petach Tikva's livestock. Uncle Avram, who was the first Jewish policeman in the settlements, mounted his horse (he was known in later years as *hazaken al ha-sus*—the old man on the horse), rode to the Arab village, challenged the robbers, allegedly killed one of them in a fight, and retrieved his village's livestock. No one ever disturbed Petach Tikva again and Uncle Avram came to be known, respected, and revered as *Sheik Ibrahim* throughout the region and the Arabian Peninsula. He was so respected that frequently Arab village leaders called upon him to help settle their disputes.

One of the reasons I have such a strong personal attachment to the State of Israel is because of my family's history there. I am also, as you know, a second cousin to Israel's President, Reuven Rivlin. I remember Ruvi (as he was called by family and friends) from that year of my rabbinic studies because I was frequently a guest at Shabbat dinner at his mother's home in Rehavia. Ruvi was then a young leader of Menachem Begin's Herut party in Jerusalem. I remember him well as a warmhearted bear of a man, decent to his core. As the state's president he has deliberately reached out to Arab Israeli citizens and pledged his support for their equal rights and equal share of Israel's resources as citizens. He is a hero to them, and he brings distinction to the office of the presidency of the Jewish state. I am proud of our family's relationship with him.

American Jewish Pride After the 1967 Six-Day War and Today

I was coming of age around the time of the 1967 Six-Day Arab-Israeli War, which cast Israel as the new David slaying the Goliath of combined Arab armies intending to destroy our young state and "push the Jews into the sea." We American Jews and world Jewry bathed in the afterglow of that lightning victory in only six days, the feeling of strength and agency it gave us. Many in my generation wanted to identify with this Israel, this amazing experience of asking no one's permission to take our place in the world. We learned Hebrew and studied the history of the state and the meaning of Zionism as the national liberation movement of the Jewish people.

We were so invested in the aspirational vision of Israel that Mom and I wanted you to have names that were interchangeable in English and Hebrew, so that as you grew up you could feel at home in America and in Israel; hence, we gave you the Biblical Hebrew names Daniel and David.

But more than 70 years into Israel's story, I know that the sense we had—and still have—of the miraculous possibilities unfolding in Israel has been clouded among many of your peers by grave concerns about the behavior of the Jewish state and its policies—particularly the injustices surrounding the Israeli government's occupation of the West Bank Palestinians, its treatment of Eritrean and Sudanese refugees, and Arab Israelis as second-class citizens despite both President Rivlin's and Prime Minister Netanyahu's efforts to raise the standard of living of Israel's Arab citizens.

I'll take up those complex issues separately, but I want to note briefly that so many Israelis, too, share these concerns and are striving to resolve them. Your help and support of our brothers and sisters in Israel who feel as we feel is a key to the nation's future and the future of the American Jewish community.

What I think it's crucial to say is that while Israel is far from meeting its aspirations to become a fully democratic society and to have peace with the Palestinians, and while it has been troubled with some of the same corrosive politics we've seen recently in the United States, it's unfair to characterize Israel as an "oppressor state" and damn it with blanket condemnations as some do on the American left—including those groups that are our traditional social justice allies.

To treat Israel as an offensive *other*—to dismiss it, say, because you might regard Benjamin Netanyahu as Israel's Donald Trump—is to push it away, and I hope you will not do that. I hope instead that you will regard Israel as part of you, one of your important and necessary homes in the world far beyond the fault lines of the current conflict—a place that can become a reliable base of belonging and connection for you as

American Jews—even if you never plan to live there yourselves. Approaching Israel in that more challenging way—from the inside instead of standing apart—means to hold it to account while feeling out, and operating from, your own resonance with the Jewish cultural, moral, and democratic values on which the nation was built. It also means developing a relationship that goes beyond received wisdom and stereotypes about Israel to get at the complexities of real life and real people in a diverse, cosmopolitan society.

It means engaging.

If you do that, you will not only enrich your understanding of Israel and yourself, but you can become an effective force for change in our community among your millennial peers. I'm not asking you to swallow your objections and blindly support Israel because that's what good Jews should do. I'm suggesting that you claim your right to help this promising, perplexing home of ours become all it can be—by at the very least supporting those groups in Israel fighting the good fight on behalf of justice, compassion, and peace. They are there—hundreds of thousands of Israelis—and one of the responsibilities we American Jews have to Israel is to lend our moral, political, and financial support to our brothers and sisters living there.

Siblings

We have a unique relationship with our people in Israel. Rabbi Donniel Hartman suggests that in this generation, Jews in Israel and America are siblings who can choose whether to return to the "house" of our parents.[4] That house is the idealized and aspirational Israel of the founding generation of the state, who hoped to create a perfect Jewish society based on the principles of justice and peace as articulated by the ancient Hebrew prophets and as written in Israel's Declaration of Independence (see the Appendix for the entire text). Jewish nationalism meant sharing a special bond with the Jewish people around the world and in Israel and spreading goodness and moral excellence so our people and the State of Israel might serve as "a light to the nations" (Isaiah 49:6).

Each child, Rabbi Hartman notes, the Israeli Jew and the American Jew, has a key to our mutual parental home, and each of us can return to it if we choose. We need to do so because we are brothers and sisters, and our two communities have much to offer each other. American liberal Jewish religious practice and creativity, volumes of Jewish scholarship and writing, Jewish art, literature, music, and film—all these have helped to create a new Diaspora Jew, one who is committed to fostering greater social justice through communal and political activism. Israel, for its part, remains a dynamic source of learning too—a second arena of Jewish creativity and an opportunity to test our people's ethical tradition while holding power and being a sovereign nation-state.

Although the ultra-Orthodox rabbinate has sought to suppress all alternatives to its interpretation of Judaism in Israel, the Israeli Reform and Conservative movements have grown dramatically in recent years and now equal 11 percent of the entire population of Israeli Jews—the same number that represent Haredi ultra-Orthodox Jews.[5] As liberal American Reform Jews, you now have a place in the conversation alongside our fellow Israeli Reform Jews.

Israel's Remarkable Diversity

So many millennial Jews who have not visited Israel do not realize how diverse a nation Israel has become and what an exciting population Israel embraces. For all the media images of right-wing settlers of European descent, Israel is, as a journalist for London's *Financial Times* put it, "a mosaic that makes European countries and some parts of the US seem homogenous."[6] Pulling in Jews from all over Europe, as well as from northern Africa, Iraq, Syria, Yemen and Ethiopia, he writes that Israeli cities have become "mélanges, where American-style shopping malls, Yemeni jewelry stores and intimate Moroccan couscous joints all seemed strangely indigenous." With the breakup of the Soviet Union, one million-plus immigrants from central Asia, Russia and Ukraine joined the mix, a crush "equivalent to 60 million immigrants arriving in the U.S." You can feel the overwhelming and enormous impact of all this and get a taste of what Israel could be—what it already is—when you visit Tel Aviv-Jaffa, a tech-fueled metro area filled not just with the beauty of the Mediterranean coast, but with art, music, and great food; a liberal, pluralistic, and democratic spirit, and an openness to diversity—to Arab and Jew, to the

LGBTQ community, to people from around the world. Or when you visit Jerusalem, a holy city to Jews, Christians, and Muslims—a rich cultural, ethnic, and religious place animated by its ancient and modern character and the intermingling of peoples from around the world.

At its best, Israel is filled with intellectual vigor, a spirit of self-criticism, and the particularly Jewish habit of constantly questioning itself and political norms. You can hear vast differences of opinion expressed constantly in the cafes and read about them everywhere. Civil discourse remains a highly valued virtue in Israel, and Israel's press is as free as any in the western world. That's not to say that there's also a growing intolerance among some sectors of the population, especially from the religious right wing that is threatened by honest criticism and debate.

The positive forces of diversity and tolerance are what you and your peers can align with and nurture in this modern and ancient nation and culture that still reaches toward its unfulfilled aspirations. I hope that you and your Israeli peers, your siblings, will find a way always to treat each other with a sense of mutual responsibility and respect in pursuit of those aspirations. I hope, as well, that we American Jews will always want to help our Israeli brothers and sisters in their times of need and that they will similarly want to help us. And I hope one more very important thing—that we can maintain our connection to Israel even when the Israeli government behaves in ways we find morally objectionable.

As brothers, you two know well that no matter how bitterly you might disagree with each other from time to time, you will always have an unbreakable bond and each of you will always be a powerful force in the life of the other. So it is, too, with you and your counterparts in Israel.

American and Israeli Aspirations

Israel isn't a perfect society, but in judging it remember America's longer history and our own struggles toward unfulfilled ideals. Remember that when the American Constitution was written, African Americans were slaves and counted as 3/5 of a person—mostly to add population strength to the smaller southern states. And women didn't have the right to vote until the beginning of the twentieth century.

The American democratic ideal was exalted, but it was and is a work in progress. America needed the Civil War to free the slaves. America needed the suffrage movement to enfranchise women. America needed the New Deal to assure a safety net for seniors and the poor. America needed the Voting Rights Act of 1965 to open the political system to African Americans. America needed Medicare for seniors, Medicaid for the poor, and Obamacare to provide healthcare to millions of people who didn't have it through employment or who couldn't afford it as individuals. America needs the Black Lives Matter movement to shine a light on lingering institutional racism. And America needs the Me Too movement to address inherent sexism and the evil of sexual assault in the home and in the workplace.

The writing of the American Constitution was an aspirational act, just as the writing of Israel's Declaration of Independence was an aspirational act. Israel doesn't have a constitution, but it has Basic Laws and it needs those Basic Laws and the Israeli court system to provide equal rights to all Israeli citizens, Jew and Arab alike. It needs a two-state solution to resolve the Israeli-Palestinian conflict and bring justice to the Palestinian people, enabling them to experience national sovereignty as a people just as we Jews do—the same sense of home that we know is so precious.

Yes, Israel is flawed just as America is flawed. But we can't abandon the struggle to help both of our homes realize our respective ideals.

Israel is a part of you as it is a part of me. Like every Jew, you have a stake and a home in the Jewish state. You don't have to believe in God to belong there. You don't have to accept the Biblical commandment as the rationale for why we need a Jewish state to identify with Israel's sense of nationhood. You already belong.

As a people we are one family. Relating to Israel is about opening our hearts to her, learning as much as we can about her, and embracing the powerful ideals on which she was founded: the vision of bringing justice and peace to the world. Working toward this goal is something we can't do without empathy and deep commitment. It means you visiting Israel as often as you can and engaging personally with Israelis. And it means for Israelis to come here and engage with us in our home as their American

Jewish siblings. Many Israelis want this. They tell me so. I certainly want it, and I hope you do as well.

Hold to the idea that our commonalities as a people, as a family, can be bigger than our differences. That's the sustaining sensibility that will lead you home.

Love,

Dad

Discussion Questions

- Where were you raised? Do you agree with the author's understanding of what constitutes a "home?"

- As a North American Jew, do you feel different from other ethnic, religious, racial, and national groups in America?

- Do you identify with the peoplehood of Israel? If so, how so?

- The author notes the impact on the American Jewish community of alt-right racist and anti-Semitic incitement and violence in Charlottesville and at the Tree of Life Synagogue in Pittsburgh. Did those events challenge your sense of America as your "home?" If so, how so?

- The author describes the relationship between Diaspora American Jews and Israelis as one of siblings. Do you regard yourself as a "sibling" to Israelis?

- The author compares the American Declaration of Independence and America's struggles with its imperfections since 1776 with the Israeli Declaration of Independence and Israel's struggle with its own imperfections since 1948. Do you believe this is an apt comparison?

Navigating Between Liberalism and Zionism

Dear Daniel and David,,

Like many liberal Jews, I was raised in an environment that was steeped in Jewish ethics, but I had very little Jewish tradition and education. We celebrated Passover and lit Hanukkah lights in my family home, but that was it. We were members of a small synagogue for one year when I was seven or eight years old, and your Uncle Michael and I attended Sunday school there; but we didn't like it, so my parents didn't insist that we continue.

I remember studying Hebrew when I was a kid with an old European rabbi (Schwartzkin was his name and I remember that his wife would call him by his last name, apparently a European custom). He was probably a Holocaust survivor but I didn't know it at the time, and he taught us in his home; but that didn't last long either.

My mother, two uncles, an aunt, and a cousin were leaders in the Los Angeles organized Jewish community, and I was proud of them for that, but it didn't affect me very much. My early Jewish experience was minimal and my Jewish self-awareness was faint.

After my father died when I was nine years old, my mother yearned for Jewish spiritual connection, so we became members of Leo Baeck Temple in Los Angeles. She was particularly drawn to Rabbi Leonard Beerman, a pacifist and human rights activist who would become a rabbinic model and a cherished friend to me.

I entered Leo Baeck's Sunday school in the 7th grade and continued into its high school program where we studied the biblical prophets, but I didn't begin to take Judaism and the Jewish experience seriously until I became a student at UC Berkeley. My own road to Zionism began with the outrage I felt after the infamous Leningrad Trials of 13 Jews who had sought to escape on a private plane from the Soviet Union to Finland after being refused exit visas to emigrate to Israel. They were arrested at the airport by the Soviet authorities in 1970, tried for treason, and sentenced to many years of hard labor. The leader was sentenced to death but when world reaction became so intensively negative, led by the United States, the USSR commuted his death sentence to life in prison.

Soviet Jews in the 1960s and 1970s might be stripped of jobs, harassed by the KGB, arrested and/or conscripted—simply for applying for permission to leave or teach Hebrew. Natan (formerly Anatoly) Sharansky was sentenced to many years of solitary confinement and became an inspiration to me as a prisoner of conscience. You can imagine how moved I was when I served as the national Chair of the Association of Reform Zionists of America (ARZA) and had a seat on the Board of Governors of the Jewish Agency for Israel that Natan chaired. Being in his presence was to be in the presence of a bona fide hero. I have a photo of him and me together near the Kotel when the JAFI Board met at that holiest site in Judaism. I told Natan that when he was a prisoner of conscience, he was one of the people who inspired me to become a rabbi and commit myself to the Jewish people. He looked me in the eye and appeared deeply moved. He said simply, "Really?" I said, "Yes!"

As I became involved in the Soviet Jewry movement on their behalf after the Leningrad Trials, I read Elie Wiesel's *Jews of Silence* which poignantly described the fear experienced by Soviet Jews since the Revolution in 1917. Our family is from that part of the world, and wanting to know more of our heritage, I took a course at the UC Berkeley Hillel on the history of the Russian Jewish community. The more I learned the more strongly I felt a connection with what was happening to Soviet Jewry in 1970 and what happened to the Jews of Europe during the Shoah. I joined the San Francisco Bay Area Council for Soviet Jewry and became an activist with the younger group called "The Soviet Jewry Action Group."

Soon after, a fellow UC student introduced me to a student group of leftist Zionist intellectuals who had formed "The Radical Jewish Union." Along with these 15 or so students, I studied and debated Zionist thought from every perspective. Given the charged political Berkeley environment in those years, I felt a natural affinity with them and with the issues with which this group grappled. Especially given the plight of Soviet Jews, we saw Zionism as our own civil rights movement. We had been involved in efforts to resist the Vietnam War and to support the civil rights of blacks in the South. Now we felt empowered to work for the rights of our own people. We could see what it meant that Jews who wanted only to live without discrimination could look to Israel for freedom, and we felt compelled to fight for them, for Israel, and to ensure and shape our own deep and lasting freedom. I was a political Zionist at that time of my life: like Theodor Herzl, I was convinced that anti-Semitism would always be with us, sometimes in egregious forms, and our best course as Jews was to give ourselves the dignity, protection and power of our own state.

I got a less intellectual and more visceral cultural sense of Jewish identity from the time I spent at a college institute run by Dr. Shlomo Bardin, a Jew from Zhitomir, Russia who spent time in Palestine before 1920. Shlomo (as we called him) met Supreme Court Justice Louis D. Brandeis, who urged him to do something on behalf of the Jewish identity of young American Jews and to help them form a bond with the people of Israel. Along with 70 college students from around the country, I spent a month immersed in Jewish culture at the Brandeis Camp Institute in Simi Valley, northwest of Los Angeles. After Shlomo's death, his name joined with Brandeis. It is now called the Brandeis-Bardin Institute and is a part of the American Jewish University.

With grounds planted with pepper, eucalyptus, citrus, and oak trees, and a very large cactus garden, the property strongly resembled Israel's terrain. We awoke each morning to Israeli music. We studied and worked together. I became an Israeli folk dancer with Dani Dassa, who brought Israeli folk dancing to Southern California. And I met Leonard (Leibel) Fein, a Jewish sociologist who inspired me then and in later years as a progressive Zionist.

Shlomo took me under his wing and invited me to come back the next summer to work on staff at the children's Camp Alonim (Hebrew for "oak trees"). From him and other mentors, I gained an appreciation of the cultural vision of Zionism that Asher Ginsburg (known by his pen name Ahad Ha-am—"one of the people") put forward in the early twentieth century, that sense of how important it is to have a place in the world that can feed and replenish the best of Jewish culture, values and tradition.

These immersions in Jewish life and philosophy were deeply defining for me, and they put me on a still unfolding path into the heart of Judaism as a Zionist and a rabbi.

A Zionism that Makes Sense for You Now

My Zionism grew from a very particular time in history. I was born a year after Israel was established and raised on "the crisis narrative" of Jewish history. The Holocaust hovered over my childhood and formative years and has been a defining experience affecting the post-war Jewish psyche. The Shoah taught Jews everywhere that powerlessness risks destruction and that the State of Israel is our surest protection against forces that would destroy us.

By the time I was 17, Israel had fought three wars. When I was 23 and living in Jerusalem, Israel was nearly overtaken in the Yom Kippur War. I understood that Israel could not lose a single war on the battlefield, that her security and survival must be the number one priority for Israelis and world Jewry, and that to ignore the real threats to the Jewish people is never an option.

I have visceral memories of seeing the footage of Palestinian terrorists in face masks at the 1972 Munich Olympics, members of the Black September terrorist organization that murdered 11 Israeli athletes, as I mentioned in an earlier letter. And I remember the persecution of the Soviet Jews that continued all the way into the 1990s.

The crisis narrative is deeply impressed on me. Yet I understand that you were not alive to have that experience of crisis; and more than that, I understand clearly the limits of thinking of Israel purely in "us against the world" survival terms. I'm not asking you to embrace fear as a reason to support Israel. I agree with Dr. Tal Becker, an associate at the Washington Institute for Near East Policy and a Fellow at the Shalom Hartman Institute in Jerusalem, who writes that the crisis narrative "is both narrow and shallow." It's narrow, he says, because the singular focus on survival and presence on the land keeps us from talking about "the breadth of what this sovereign project might offer for the collective Jewish experience." And it's shallow because "it pursues Jewish survival for its own sake but tells no deeper story as to why that survival is important and worth fighting for." [1]

So what kind of conversation can we have about Israel today that is broad and visionary enough to talk about how the Jewish State could be a source of sustenance, connection and renewal for all Jews, and even for the world? How do we begin to articulate—to ourselves and then to the wider world—why Israel matters and why we are willing to fight for it?

Dr. Becker argues that in order to build a conversation that achieves a vision of Jewish unity behind an Israel we can support wholeheartedly, we need to focus on values. We need to ask ourselves and each other what it will take to address Israel's challenges and build a moral and just society in which the policies, politics and culture reflect our Jewish values, tradition and experience as a people.

For those operating strictly out of the crisis mindset, Jewish unity is defined narrowly by who stands with us against common threats. But the values narrative that Becker advocates defines Jewish unity in terms of a moral engagement that we share—not because we agree or because the one overriding issue confronting us is survival, but because we're committed to engage in a complicated, divisive, agonizing, and exhilarating process of writing together the next chapter of Jewish history. When we do that, we become worthy of the better angels in our tradition and our historic experience.

This is a visionary conversation I believe you as representatives of the millennial generation can come to with passion. We're seeing many groups in the Diaspora take the lead in pursuing opposition to the occupation and fighting for social justice for women, African refugees, and Palestinian Arab-Israeli citizens. In this powerful drive for justice, I believe it's also necessary to give voice and respect to the hundreds of thousands of Jewish Israelis who long for peace, safety and equality for all in the place that's not only their home, but our cultural home as well. It's home to Jews from around the world who have sought refuge, connection and a future there. We need to let our clarity about what we oppose lead us to what we hope for, aspire to, and embrace as Jews—and how we can help make it a reality in Israel.

It's extremely difficult to find the balance between our particular Jewish interests—the concerns and identity we have as a nation and a "tribe"—and our universal concerns for ethics, democracy, and the wellbeing of all. We liberals in the Diaspora are schooled in accommodation, and less comfortable asserting our own rights. Yet the tension between the particular and the universal, the tribal and the humanitarian, runs throughout Jewish tradition. All of us, Diaspora Jews and Israelis, need to navigate it here in a values-based discussion about what Israel should be. If we can do that, a new Zionist paradigm will emerge that reflects a new stage in Zionist, Israeli, and Jewish history.

We have had iteration upon iteration of Zionism. Theodor Herzl's political Zionism envisioned Israel as a solution to the problem of anti-Semitism. Ahad Ha-am's cultural Zionism regarded Zionism as a way to mend Jewish alienation from the spirit of Judaism. Chaim Weizmann's practical Zionism synthesized political and cultural Zionism. Zionism took a socialist turn with David Ben Gurion's Labor Zionism, and shifted toward the Torah and rabbinic law with Rav Abraham Isaac Kook's religious version. Vladimir Jabotinsky and Menachem Begin added a tribal militancy to the political-cultural models with their revisionist Zionism. And today, sadly, what dominates Israel is an even more militant right-wing, extremist, anti-democratic, and nativist Zionism: the "Israel must dominate" model.

What I believe Israel needs now is Tal Becker's model: values-based Aspirational Zionism.

What is Aspirational Zionism?

Aspirational Zionism requires us personally and collectively to ground ourselves in our values. It insists that we apply those values to our engagement with Israel, grappling with such questions as:

- How do our liberal Jewish values augment Israel's democratic, diverse, and pluralistic society?
- How do we bring the moral aspirations of the Biblical prophets and the compassionate impulses of the Talmudic rabbis—our ethical history—into contemporary ethical challenges like Israel's relationship with the Palestinians and with Arab Israelis?

- How do we join our fellow Jews in Israel and around the world to fight our enemies—without sacrificing our Jewish moral sensibilities and democratic values?
- How do we as a people genuinely pursue peace as a moral and quintessentially Jewish obligation despite the threat of terror and war?
- How do we support Israelis while advocating on behalf of democracy and the equal rights and dignity of Israel's minorities?
- How do we oppose oppressive Israeli policies without turning our opponents into the "other," and losing the possibility for common ground—true peace?
- How do we preserve a Jewish majority in Israel while supporting social justice, a shared society with Arab Israeli citizens, and the human rights of all?

These questions take us to the heart of our liberal and Reform beliefs and bring them into the real world, where we can take a turn at making them compatible with a liberal, democratic nationalism.

Nationalism has lately become shorthand for self-interested exclusion, oppression, and boasts of supremacy, but democratic nations are what we make them. Many of us saw the promise of our nation in Obama's America, and we fight for our vision of what America can be as we struggle against a surge of anti-democratic forces today following Donald Trump. We can do the same in our relationship with the State of Israel. We can insist on and fight for an Israel that lives up to its founding principles of democracy, justice, peace, and the full expression of our highest Jewish values; an Israel that reflects the best of our Jewish culture and tradition.

We liberal American Jews can be fully Zionist even as we ask the hard questions that go to the core of Jewish tradition itself. We can do the hard work of bridging the tribal and the universal, addressing our need as Jews for sovereignty and rights as a nation, as well as the needs and rights of all.

Zionism is personal to me for all the reasons I've mentioned, and this you know because you've lived with me and know me as few people in the world do. I know you'll face many of the same struggles with it that I have. At the early stages of my engagement with Zionism in Berkeley, it was not a huge leap from being a humanitarian activist to becoming involved with a group of socialist-Zionist students. But being a Zionist got more complicated when, in later years, I encountered the Orthodox right-wing settler groups that disregard the rights and aspirations of the Palestinian people. Their Zionism is not my Zionism.

I have learned that I can and must stand with a Zionism that holds Israel to its highest visions. Before we can hope to bring peace and justice to the world, we have to find a way to do it at home, with our Jewish cultural family in Israel.

Issues of Life and Death

Rabbi Leonard Beerman, my childhood rabbi, was a great rabbinic figure, a giant of moral conscience, and as eloquent a speaker and compelling a story-teller as I have ever known. I felt privileged that he wanted to know me in his later years, and I enjoyed our frequent lunches together.

The last lunch we shared before he died was in August 2014 following the second Gaza War. The High Holidays were approaching and both Leonard and I planned to speak about the war and its impact on Israel and the Jewish people. Both of us were struggling, but in very different ways. I supported Israel's right to fight in that war, but he was dead set against it and intended to say so to his community.

Leonard was a pacifist who came to this position after serving as a Marine during World War II and participating in Israel's 1948 War of Independence. At our last lunch together, he referred me to the passage in Dostoyevsky's *The Brothers Karamazov* in which a conversation takes place between two of the three brothers, Alyosha and Ivan.

"Alyosha was a good, pure, gentle, and loving man," Leonard quoted from memory. "He was poor and humble, and he inspired love in everyone around him. He loved humankind and felt God's grace in everyone he met."

Leonard recounted a part of the story in which Ivan asked Alyosha if he would tolerate the torture of a single child if it meant peace and tranquility for humanity as a whole. Alyosha said he would because saving as many lives as possible far outweighs the life of even one child.[2]

Ivan said he would have saved that one child even if it meant sacrificing the many adults whom he believed were corrupt.

Leonard asked me to consider this story in light of the loss of innocent life in the Gaza War. As we parted, we wished each other good luck in writing our sermons, and he said: "John, remember to be moral!" Though I did not ask him specifically, I was fairly certain that he sided with Ivan, while I sided with Alyosha.

The 2014 Gaza War

As I wrote my sermon, Leonard's moral conscience infused my thinking, but I was not him and could not take the position he took. I supported Israel's right to defend itself against Hamas' firing of 10,000 missiles over a number of years against Israeli civilian communities even though I knew that innocent people, including children, would be injured and killed in Gaza. It tore at my heart and conscience to support it, but I knew that Hamas deliberately situated itself in civilian areas, in schools and hospitals, in residential neighborhoods, and in apartment buildings so it could draw fire from Israel and then accuse Israel of committing crimes against humanity in wars that Hamas had provoked.

I believe that a nation has a moral duty to protect its citizens, and even though the loss of life in that war was the greatest of tragedies, I supported Israel's right to self-defense.

Leonard took the opposite position and expressed his deep concern about the cost of Israel's retaliation against Hamas. Leonard never shied away from controversy—even in his last sermon, which this proved to be. His *Los Angeles Times* obituary recounts how he was in great pain as he forcefully opposed the war and told his congregation that the Israel Defense Forces had shown "callous disregard" for the lives of those in Gaza. Though his words angered many, and there would be vehement disagreement afterward, most of his congregants at Leo Baeck Temple rose at the end to give him a standing ovation.[3]

The aspiration in Aspirational Zionism is not for an end to disagreement and passionate debate. It's precisely the clash of our opinions and our willingness to understand each other—influence each other, listen to each other—that is what will shape our Zionism and Israel going forward. There's room in Aspirational Zionism for all of us—the spectrum from

Leonard to me, to you—as we grapple with our values on the level of life and death while holding a vision of what Israel is and can be.

Peoplehood and Universalism—Zionism and Liberalism

Elie Wiesel said once that no human being speaks generally or universally. Every human being speaks in a particular language and from a particular experience. Each of us belongs to some tribal group, to a community, a nation, and to a people. I love John Lennon's song "Imagine" but I don't accept the premise that we strive to live beyond national and religious identities.

It's critically important to be able to navigate between the often conflicting liberal prophetic values upon which American Reform Judaism was established, and Zionism, the national philosophy of Jewish peoplehood.

As liberal Reform aspirational Zionists, our liberalism demands acceptance of the *other*—even as we insist on our national rights and puzzle out how to claim them in a moral fashion. It's difficult to hold onto each pole in tension, but hold them we must for the sake of the full expression of our Jewish identity.

Love,

Dad

Discussion Questions:

- The author describes briefly the different approaches to Zionism since Theodor Herzl convened the World Zionist Congress in Basel, Switzerland in 1897 (e.g., political, cultural, pragmatic, labor, revisionist, religious, and right-wing settler Zionism). Which of these Zionist approaches most resonate with you?

- The author presents "Aspirational Zionism." What is your reaction to this approach in comparison with the other approaches?

- The author discusses his childhood Rabbi Leonard Beerman's 2014 High Holiday sermon following the 2014 Gaza War, in which he was highly critical of Israel's conduct of the war. Do you agree or disagree with Rabbi Beerman? Why?

- Do you believe that liberal Jewish values and national Zionist values can be integrated?

Why Reform Zionism Matters

Dear Daniel and David,

What is Reform Zionism, and why should you care? These two questions are more important than you may think, and they are now what I want now to consider with you. I believe that Reform Zionism as a movement offers American liberal Jews a way to engage personally with Israel and with Israelis that's consistent with our liberal American Jewish values.

I make this a point now in particular because for many American liberal Jews, "Zionism" has become a dirty word. With this more common perception, it's important to understand why Zionism has come to be understood this way by so many people.

Zionism has acquired a bad name for a number of reasons. One is that "Zionist" is increasingly associated with right-wing Jewish support of the current right-wing Israeli government's settlement enterprise, and its disregard for the right of the Palestinian people to self-determination in a state of their own.

What is Reform Zionism?

Both Zionism and Reform Judaism are radical reactions to the preceding two thousand years of Jewish history. Each emerged during the nineteenth century in Europe.

Classical Zionism is a product of nineteenth century European nationalism.

Classical Reform Judaism is a product of the nineteenth century European Enlightenment.

Today both Zionism and Reform Judaism have evolved dramatically from their respective origins. Reform Zionism offers liberal American Jews a movement in which we can actively support Israel as a democratic Jewish state and still be true to our own American liberal values.

The Israeli Reform Movement Today

The Israeli Reform movement grew slowly. In its early years it depended for its funding upon the generosity of world Jewry. So far the Israeli government has not officially recognized it as a legitimate Jewish religious stream deserving of funding.

The movement, however, has developed rapidly over the past decade. Today, our Israeli Reform movement includes:

- 50 Reform congregations placed strategically around the country
- a full Rabbinic seminary (Hebrew Union College in Jerusalem)
- 100 ordained Israeli Reform rabbis 30 more students training to become rabbis in the next few years
- two Reform kibbutzim (Lotan and Yahel in the south)
- Leo Baeck High School in Haifa
- several Reform public elementary schools
- an active Reform youth movement called Noar Telem
- pre-army programs for high school graduatesan
- Israeli Religious Action Center (IRAC—the social justice arm of Israel's Reform movement—that fights on behalf of religious pluralism, democracy, and humanitarian causes, and argues against racism and misogyny before the government and courts)
- dozens of local social action projects in Reform congregations that fight against hunger and poverty, on behalf of women's and LGBTQ rights, in favor of African refugee asylum, economic justice, and a shared society with Arab Israeli citizens
- thousands of life-cycle events (baby namings and *brit milah, b'nai mitzvah*, conversions, weddings, and funerals) performed by Israeli Reform rabbis

The Israeli Reform movement is winning battle after battle in the courts on behalf of religious pluralism and democracy in the state, and it is winning the hearts and minds of large numbers of non-Orthodox Israelis. Many Israelis are attracted to our movement's egalitarian prayer and holiday celebrations, our non-Orthodox liberal Jewish values, and a place to raise their children according to what they believe.

What Does This all Mean for American Reform Jews?

As you know, I served as the national Chairperson of the Association of Reform Zionists of America (ARZA), the Zionist arm of 1.5 million American Reform Jews, between 2016 and 2018. I met many Israeli Reform Rabbis, our movement's lay leadership in Israel and in the international Reform Zionist movement (ARZENU); and I can tell you that our leadership includes many extraordinary people—inspired, moral, and decent. I came to appreciate the role that Reform Zionism plays as a counterbalance to right-wing Zionism and Israel's current government's right-wing policies. Reform Zionism offers both a philosophy and a movement with which you both and your peers can become a part.

Jewish Demographics in 2050

That being said, I am worried; I want to explain why by citing the future of Jewish demographics over the next generation.

First, it's important to say that we Jews have always stressed quality over quantity. We are a small people and religious group relative to Christianity and Islam, each of which claims over one billion adherents. We Jews share some things in common with these two great monotheistic religions: an ethical tradition and faith in one God. But we're fundamentally different because we Jews are a people and a civilization with a history, land, language(s), faith, literature, law, lore, and culture. That being said, it's important to note that the demography of world Jewry is rapidly changing—and we ignore those changes at our peril.

Professor Sergio Della Pergola is an Italian-born Israeli demographer and statistician. He projects that, given a median fertility rate, the world Jewish population in 2050 will be 14,481,000. This projection is based on the traditional definition of a Jew as one born of a Jewish mother, or one who converts to Judaism. That figure does not include patrilineal Jews (Reform Judaism in the United States recognizes Jews born of a Jewish father who practices Judaism), or the non-Jewish partners and spouses of Jews who identify with the Jewish community and participate in Jewish home and synagogue practice. These people add another two to four million people to Della Pergola's figures.

Della Pergola predicts an intriguing distribution of the world's Jews in the not-too-distant future:

- 8,230,000 Jews will live in Israel (57 percent of world Jewry)
- 6,251,000 Jews will live in the Diaspora (43 percent)
- of the Diaspora population, 5,036,000 will live in the U.S. and Canada (35 percent)
- 1,160,000 Jews will live in other Diaspora lands (8 percent)

This means that for the first time since the beginning of the modern Zionist movement, more than half of Jews in the world will live in Israel.[1]

The Peoplehood of Israel

Why is this important?

Daniel and David—Each of you has a strong Jewish identity and you care about the State of Israel. I'm not at all worried about your personal attachment to the Jewish people. However, I am worried about the lack of affinity to Israel felt by many of your American millennial peers. A bond or lack of a bond that they feel with the peoplehood of Israel will determine the future of the American Jewish community in its relationship to the people and State of Israel. This concern is one of the main reasons I'm writing these letters to you and your peers.

If the bond with the Jewish people diminishes in strength with your generation and the generations to come after you, the tendency will be greater for Jews to assimilate and/or cease being Jewish altogether. The faith of the Jewish people is no longer adequate to sustain Judaism from generation to generation. But the feeling of being part of the Jewish people can sustain Jewish continuity.

There are many practices that define the Jewish people. They include wearing a kippah and tallit during prayer, keeping kosher, celebrating Shabbat, learning Hebrew, and giving children Hebrew names.

Among the most important things that can inspire the sense of peoplehood in Jews is visiting, living in, and/or making aliyah to Israel. For 2,000 years, Jews yearned to return to our ancestral homeland. Today we can do so from anywhere in the world, and we can form friendships with Israelis that tie our two major Jewish communities together as one people.

Our identity as a people is arguably the most critical element that will sustain American Jewry over the long term. Our study of Torah and celebration of holidays and life-cycle events are important to our Jewish identity and the strengthening of the Jewish family. But it's our sense of peoplehood—through our engagement with the people and State of Israel—that can truly transmit what is essential in the modern Jewish experience. The leadership of the Israeli Reform movement has told me that they need us American Jews at least as much as we need them.

What We Liberal Reform Zionists Have to Offer Israel

We American Reform Zionists have much to offer our Israeli Reform brothers and sisters and the State of Israel as a whole. As liberal American Jews, we've been schooled in a nation in which religious diversity is a hallmark of our culture. Israel, though assuring freedom of religion for all its inhabitants, has failed to assure religious freedom to one group: non-Orthodox Jews.

Israel protects the holy sites of all religious faiths and supports and encourages those religions to thrive in Israel; all except for one group: non-Orthodox Jews.

The Chief Rabbinate of the State of Israel recognizes the legitimacy of only Orthodox and ultra-Orthodox Judaism. Only Orthodox and ultra-Orthodox communities receive generous Israeli taxpayer support to sustain their rabbis, synagogues, communities, and schools—despite the fact that only 20-25% of Israeli citizens are Orthodox.

It's infuriating to me that the only remaining oppressed Jewish group in the world is non-Orthodox Jewry living in the State of Israel.

The Battle for the Soul of Israel

There's a battle raging for the soul of Israel between the ultra-Orthodox and the non-Orthodox communities; between the political right and the political left; between tyranny and democracy. To preserve liberal Jewish values and democratic traditions in the state, Israel needs a healthy synthesis between Judaism and Zionism and between liberalism and Jewish peoplehood. I believe that Reform Zionism and Reform Judaism offer that synthesis.

Why?

Because we Reform Jews bring to Zionism and the Jewish State a tradition of non-coercive liberal Jewish thought and practice.

We American Reform Jews understand the benefits that accrue to all religions when church and state are separate.

We American Reform Jews know that diversity of opinion enriches everyone.

We grasp how all the religious streams (e.g., Orthodox, Conservative, Reform, Reconstructionist, and Renewal) have thrived in America because they've been free to pursue their own truths and develop their communities and practices without interference from the government or an official state rabbinate.

We need Israeli Reform Judaism to succeed, and Israeli Reform Judaism needs American Reform Judaism to reach its full potential.

I've found great satisfaction and learned much through my engagement with Reform Zionism, in my relationship with our Reform Israeli and international partners, and in being part of the Jewish people.

Rabbi Josh Weinberg, the Reform movement's Vice President for Reform Zionism and Israel and the Executive Director of ARZA, with whom I have worked so closely over a period of years, put it well with these words:

"Israel is the grand stage on which Jewish values, ideas, hopes, and aspirations are played out over a political landscape, presenting the opportunity to take a biblical promise and turn it into a modern-day reality. The Reform Movement is committed to helping to shape that reality, promoting our shared values of acceptance and pluralism in Israel."[2]

I challenge you to engage with it!

Love,

Dad

Discussion Questions:

- What do you believe the American liberal Jewish experience can offer Israelis in the area of religious practice and attitudes toward the separation of church and state?

- Many American Jews consider Judaism to be primarily a religion, but the author suggests that Judaism (per Rabbi Mordecai Kaplan) is a civilization; and that the land of Israel, the peoplehood of Israel, and the State of Israel ought to be integral to the identity of the American Jew. Do you agree or disagree?

The International Campaign Against Israel

Dear Daniel and David,

"Zionism is genocide!"

"Israel is an apartheid state!"

I'm sure you've heard these incendiary statements tossed into conversations about the Israeli-Palestinian situation, and I know it can be hard to know what to think or how to respond when you do hear it. So in this letter I am going to offer you insights into where this language comes from and about the interlinked campaigns to attack Israel's legitimacy that they reflect.

First, some background. The international community often asks Israel to conduct itself according to an unrealistic, unfair standard of behavior that sometimes crosses the line into anti-Semitism. I dislike focusing on this kind of unfairness as much as I suspect you dislike hearing about it; but it's important to understand specifically how this ongoing, institutionally sanctioned campaign to shame and discredit Israel has developed, and what its true aims are.

Doing that requires my teasing apart the two ideas that have become falsely and damagingly fused in these arguments against Israel. The first is a reasonable one: Israel ought to aspire to uphold international standards of human rights and be held accountable for doing it. That's as true for Israel as for every other country in the world. The second part of the equation, however, brings in a toxic corollary that's only applied to the Jewish state: If Israel doesn't perfectly meet those standards, then it doesn't deserve to exist as an independent nation.

Because this twinned argument has in some cases become institutionalized, Israel, unlike any other country in the world, is forced to defend its existence on an ongoing basis. The disturbing, unacceptable truth is that in this situation, Jews are not granted the power, pride, agency, and cultural self-worth that come with nationhood. Because of this ongoing campaign, we have to keep asserting our worth, our right to self-deter-mination, and our people's equal and legitimate standing in the world.

The separate and unequal treatment we face is unacceptable.

What Exactly is the Movement Against Israel and What Does it Seek to Do?

The campaign that argues that the Jewish people have no right to a state of our own sits alongside conventional warfare and terrorism as part of the battle against Israel that's been waged since the state was established in 1948.

A loosely coordinated group including the International Palestinian solidarity movement, left-wing political activists, American and Euro-pean academicians, and overt and covert anti-Semites practice this quieter form of attack in diplomatic circles, academia, the international media, and polite society. Confusingly, some members of this group are people we liberal Jews consider allies on other fronts—even those we join regularly to battle the injustices facing them.

These groups base their argument on the premise that the State of Israel's existence can't be justified morally, because it's built on stolen territory. They assert that Israel doesn't have the moral right to defend itself when attacked. Then, in applying rules and standards of conduct to the government of Israel that they don't apply to other nations, critics seek to turn Israel into a pariah state, and they advocate the same fate that befell the former Apartheid South African regime through boycotts, divestments and sanctions (i.e., the BDS Movement).

While some of these groups are outright Holocaust deniers (the most vicious form of anti-Semitism), others claim that the Palestinian people shouldn't have to suffer because the Jews were victims of the Holocaust, an argument that's a gross over-simplification of a partial truth.

Jews have lived in the land of Israel continuously for 3,600 years, since the time of the Biblical Abraham and Sarah. In the modern period, they began populating Palestine long before the Holocaust.

The Holocaust was not a factor in the development of the Zionist dream that began in the late nineteenth century. Zionism flowed, instead, from a desire to create a national home for the Jewish people whose collective identity encompasses a way of life spanning religion, ritual, law, ethics, language, history, politics, and culture. As Einat Wilf, an Israeli politician and feminist activist, explains, "In a world where nations and peoples were increasingly considered to possess a universal right to sovereignty in states of their own, where they could enjoy liberty and dignity, free from the oppressions of empire, the Jewish nation [declared that it] possessed that right as well." [1]

It's beyond question that Jewish immigration to Palestine intensified in the 1930s after Hitler's rise to power in Germany, and the murder of six million Jews inspired sympathy for the Jewish people that led to the United Nations 1947 Partition resolution. Jews had few safe places in the world, and the international community rightly supported a move to create a permanent home and haven for them in Palestine.

Given that opening, Zionists took the revolutionary step of saying yes to sovereignty and yes to freedom from oppression, rejecting a destiny of victimhood and making us, the Jewish people, agents of our own liberation. Revolutions aren't polite or passive. They massively disrupt the status quo. It's worth remembering that in the creation of Israel, huge—and approximately equal—numbers of people were displaced on both sides. About 750,000 Palestinians either fled or were forced to leave the lands they'd called home when the state was declared. At the same time, about 750,000 Jews who had lived in surrounding Arab and Muslim lands for centuries were forced to leave their homes and flee to Israel. The lives of two populations were upended, with no compensation for losses on either side.

In an ideal situation, each side would have been resettled and absorbed into the reconfigured map, with subsequent generations claiming their new locales as home. But that, of course, isn't what happened. Instead we have an ongoing Palestinian refugee and human-rights crisis and an Israeli-Palestinian conflict that seems never to end.

The campaign against Israel tacitly assumes that all will be well if only we Jews cede our sovereignty to our declared antagonists and go back to victim status, restoring the historic power imbalance that held us down for millennia. As a small minority in Arab lands, we know well that that is what will happen if a *one state for two peoples* plan comes to pass and

Palestinian Arabs become the majority in Israel, as the coalition opposing the Jewish State hopes will happen.

It's imperative to criticize Israel's sometimes egregious behavior toward Palestinians inside and outside its borders, and to fight for accountability and change. But it's unreasonable in the extreme to suggest that the only way to achieve that change is to dissolve the sovereign Jewish state and ask us once again to embrace victimhood. Yet that's the underlying goal of all the rhetoric leveled against Israel by delegitimizers.

The "Zionism is Racism" Argument

The United Nations took a particularly pointed stance against Israel when, in 1975, the Arab and Soviet block of nations passed a resolution that equated Zionism with racism.[2] Though it was rescinded in 1991[3] as a condition insisted upon by Israel before the Jewish state participated in the historic Madrid Peace Conference—in which Israel faced all its Arab neighbors and the leaders of the Palestinians around a conference table for the first time—the label equating Zionism with racism had already stuck in the imagination of millions of people around the world.

More recently, that same terminology was used against Israel by the international Palestinian solidarity movement in its Boycott, Divestiture, and Sanctions (BDS) campaign. The BDS movement took a page out of the playbook of the international campaign that successfully helped to change the racist Apartheid government of South Africa into a democracy led by Nelson Mandela in 1991.

It's important to assess honestly the relationship between Israel and the Palestinians. There's violence between the two sides. There's terror. There are human rights abuses and deep injustice in Israel's treatment of Palestinians. But there's no genocide and no apartheid. Those are slanderous words of propaganda, the aim of which isn't justice, but rather the stripping of a people—our people—of the sovereignty we've demanded for ourselves.

There must be reparations paid to the Palestinians just as reparations need to be paid to the 700,000 Jews who lost everything when they fled Arab nations after the establishment of the State of Israel after 1948—and there must also be equal rights for all. That will only be possible if each people has its own state.

The "Israel is an Apartheid State" Argument

The international Palestinian solidarity movement seeks to pound Israel by equating the racist Apartheid regime of the former South African racist government with Israel in its policies toward Palestinians living in Israel and the West Bank. It has gone so far as to advocate bringing charges of war crimes and genocide against Israel's politicians, diplomats, and officers of the Israeli Defense Forces. But even a cursory comparison between the old South African Apartheid regime and the democratic State of Israel negates the equivalence.

Rabbi Warren Goldstein, a former Chief Rabbi of South Africa, wrote:

"...Israel has no Population Registration Act, no Group Areas Act, no Mixed Marriages and Immorality act, no Separate Representation of Voters Act, no Separate Amenities Act, no pass laws or any of the myriad apartheid laws. To the contrary, Israel is a vibrant liberal democracy and accords full political, religious and other human rights to all its peoples, including its more than one million Arab citizens, many of whom hold positions of authority including that of cabinet minister, Member of Parliament, and judge at every level, including that of the Supreme Court. All citizens vote on the same roll in regular, multiparty elections. There are Arab parties and Arab members of other parties in Israel's parliament. Arabs and Jews share all public facilities, including hospitals and malls, buses, cinemas and parks, universities and cultural [venues]." [4]

Rabbi Goldstein's statements are true; but that isn't to say that Arab citizens of Israel enjoy the same benefits and rights that Israeli Jews enjoy, such as equal access to government funds and services, and the right to live anywhere in the State of Israel. This must be addressed if Israel is to maintain its democratic traditions. Thankfully, the President of the State of Israel, Reuven Rivlin, has publicly called for more public services and support for Israeli Palestinian communities in the state. Prime Minister Benjamin Netanyahu echoed these calls. Over the past five years, policies have been put in place to make available to the Arab citizens of Israel more funds and services. The test will be, in the end, how well and how quickly the Arab Israeli community rises in education, employment, income, and engagement with Israel as a whole.

Palestinian Arabs living in the West Bank, however, are not Israeli citizens; they do not enjoy the same protections, rights, and privileges as do those living in Israel as Israeli citizens. For West Bank Palestinian Arabs, the fight is and always has been one against occupation. Many Jews don't like that claim, but it's a legitimate one born of a century of neglect by Arab and world powers that callously used the local Arab population as game pieces on a shifting board of changing geopolitical aims.

The "Jews were never there" Argument

Some anti-Israel groups aim to make Israel seem to be an illegitimate rogue state by erasing the Jewish connection with the Biblical land of Israel, despite volumes of Biblical and written historical references and archaeological evidence. They consider Jewish immigration to Palestine, now Israel, the result of nineteenth century European colonialism, thus implying that Zionism is a falsehood, and that Jews have no historic ties to the land.

A sampling of the argument:

• In October 2010, Al-Mutawakel Taha of the Palestinian Authority's information Ministry, speaking in his official capacity, published a paper that denied any Jewish connection to the Western Wall of the Second Temple and stated that "the Al Buraq Wall [named for the donkey that brought Muhammed to the Wall before his ascent to heaven in the prophet's dream vision] is the western wall of Al Aqsa and has no religious significance to Jews." Palestinian officials have often rejected claims of Jewish heritage in Jerusalem and claim that the "Wall" is part of "occupied" east Jerusalem.

• On February 26, 2012, Palestinian Authority President Mahmoud Abbas, speaking in Qatar at an Arab League conference, also challenged the historical Jewish connection to Jerusalem.[5] The denial of history was repeated three years later by Sheikh Muhammad Ahmad Hussein, the grand mufti of Jerusalem, who claimed that a Jewish temple never existed on the Temple Mount.[6]

• In October 2010, UNESCO, the United Nations Educational, Scientific and Cultural Organization, endorsed the Palestinian Authority's demand that Rachel's Tomb outside of Bethlehem, long a revered Jewish pilgrimage site, not only be removed from Israel's declared historic sites but actually be declared a mosque. Even Yasser Arafat didn't make such a claim until 1996. UNESCO declared as well that Israel can't claim the Cave of the Machpelah in Hebron, the traditional burial site of the biblical forebears of the Jewish people (Genesis 23) as a national heritage site.

Such statements are political, not historical.

The "Apartheid Wall" vs "The Security Fence"

A potent symbol of the oppression facing Palestinians is the security fence placed on Israel's border in the West Bank, often referred to as the "Apartheid Wall" (only 4% is a wall and the rest is a fence). Although it was built to stop Palestinian terrorists and suicide bombers from entering Israel after 2002, the tragedy is that there's truth to the charge that the fence has caused disruption and injustice for Palestinians. Its installation has torn up ancestral land plots, cut down olive groves (the main cash crop for Palestinian farmers), isolated villages, and brought added misery to the lives of Palestinians.

The fence, however, has been effective in fulfilling its primary purpose: not one suicide bomber or terrorist has infiltrated Israel from the West Bank since it was completed. But retired Colonel Danny Tirza, the head of Military Administration that planned and established the fence, will be happy to see it come down. When he led my synagogue group and me on a tour of the security fence, he told us that he personally looked forward to being the one to begin tearing down this fence once a peace agreement is signed between Israel and the Palestinians. The uncomfortable, twofold truth is this: The fence is awful, and it saves lives.

The Black Lives Matter Movement and Intersectionality

The Black Lives Matter (BLM) Movement, founded in 2013, more recently evoked and intensified the "Zionism is racism" slander in the context of a new movement based on the principle of "intersectionality."

The Movement for Black Lives Matter Platform, released in the summer of 2015, generally condemns in the United States racism—overt and covert—in health care, police and criminal justice, education, employment, income disparity, banking, business, and housing. It describes the systemic range of injustices committed in this country not only against people of color, but also against women, the LGBTQ community, and the poor. It presents more than 40 policy recommendations, including an overhaul of our criminal justice system and prisons, the decriminalization of black youth, abolition of the death penalty, and reparations for slavery to the African American community—specifically in the areas of health care and higher education.

This 40,000-word document, endorsed by 70 African American organizations representing thousands of African Americans across the country, is a crushing indictment of American white society and institutions.

A few sentences toward the end of the document stunned the pro-Israel community in a section called "Invest-Divest." There it's written:

"The US justifies and advances the global war on terror via its alliance with Israel and is complicit in the genocide taking place against the Palestinian people…Israel is an apartheid state."

Many American Jews were so offended by the BLM platform's anti-Israel statements that they urged pulling out of any coalition that includes groups that are openly anti-Israel. Though I understand this response and emotionally feel it's justified, the challenge to American Jewish identity and dignity is complicated and emotionally wrought—especially for liberal Jewish activists who identify with the broader aims of the BLM movement. And so I want to spend some time discussing why I believe withdrawing is a mistake. But first, I want to discuss *intersectionality*. A blog post published in 2017 by YWBoston explains:

Intersectionality is considered crucial to social equity work. Activists and community organizations are calling for and participating in more dynamic conversations about the differences in experience among people with different overlapping identities. Without an intersectional lens, events and movements that aim to address injustice towards one group may end up perpetuating systems of inequities towards other groups. Intersectionality …encourages nuanced conversations around inequity…It enlightens us to health disparities among women of color, provides pathways for our youth leaders to understand identity, and is crucial to the advocacy work we support.

Our synagogue's social justice task force aligns itself with this *intersectional* work even though we're identified as a strongly pro-Israel community. We've taken this decision because we believe that linking ourselves to coalitions throughout the Los Angeles area is consistent with our mission to advocate on behalf of criminal justice reform, the elimination of poverty, affordable housing, and other matters on the national Reform movement's social justice agenda. I want to acknowledge that those with whom we are working are people of good will from across the religious, socio-economic, ethnic, and gender divide in the greater Los Angeles area.

Given those few sentences in the BLM Platform that are clearly anti-Semitic, our being part of such a diverse movement carries a measure of risk for us as Jews. But we deliberately chose to remain engaged in BLM for reasons of enlightened self-interest. On the one hand, the BLM comports with our Reform Jewish values against discrimination of all kinds; and on the other, it's important to be in a position in which we can educate our intersectional partners about Judaism, liberal Zionism, and the State of Israel.

In March 2017, Collier Meyerson wrote in *The Nation* that that year's International Women's Strike day of action "took an anti-colonial, anti-imperialist position, calling for the destruction of walls "from Mexico to Palestine."

As occurred with the Black Lives Matter Platform's anti-Israel comments, once again, we liberal Jews and Zionists confronted our intersectional partners' anti-Israel and anti-Zionist attitudes.

Meyerson noted that "Organizers of the strike wrote in its platform that the decolonization of Palestine is 'the beating heart of this new feminist movement.'"

In response, "*Bustle*" politics editor Emily Shire, writing in a *New York Times* op-ed, expressed her dismay over the platform's stance on Israel. Shire said she felt she was being forced to "sacrifice" her Zionism for the sake of her feminism. She argued that "Regardless of your opinion on BDS, it has nothing to do with feminism."

Palestinian feminist Linda Sarsour chimed in and asserted that you can't be a Zionist feminist because Palestinian women live under the Israeli military occupation in the West Bank.

Shire countered that to single out Israel and Zionism as the culprit against women's issues is unwarranted and confuses the international feminist movement.

The reaction in the wider Jewish community was swift—reflecting a fear that other Palestinian-American feminists have assumed leadership roles in American social-justice movements and have introduced the Palestinian issue into intersectional activism and politics. These pro-Israel voices worry that many liberal young people and people of color in the United States will turn against Israel.

Brad Lander—a member of the New York City Council from Brooklyn, a Jew and a Zionist—defended Linda Sarsour, whom he knows personally. Lander said although Sarsour is an anti-Zionist, she is not an anti-Semite. He said that Sarsour has stood up for the Jewish community against anti-Semitic hate crimes and has worked with Jews for Racial and Economic Justice. The American Jewish right wing, nevertheless, demonized her as an enemy of the Jewish people.

When Anti-Zionism is Anti-Semitism

This raises the question: can a person be anti-Zionist and anti-Israel and not be anti-Semitic? My own view is that if people hold Israel to an unfair standard of behavior that they don't hold for any other nation, or if people believe that Israel doesn't have a right to exist, that is anti-Semitism. If, however, someone is critical of policies of the State of Israel, especially with regard to the occupation of the Palestinians in the West Bank, that is not necessarily anti-Semitism.

Many right-wing Jewish pro-Israel activists equate anti-Zionism with anti-Semitism, but it isn't necessarily so. Being part of the intersectional movement and in coalition with others gives liberal Reform Zionists the opportunity to defend Israel's legitimacy as a Jewish State when it's attacked and/or criticized without sacrificing our liberal values.

Being a Zionist these days is challenging. When Israel or Zionism is criticized and attacked, on the one hand we find ourselves in a defensive position; and on the other, we need to make the argument that Zionism isn't monolithic in philosophy and politics and that liberal Zionism enables one to be pro-Israel and true to one's liberal Jewish values.

What Do We Do Now?

Many take the position that offense is the best defense, that showing any sign of weakness signals defeat, and that there's only one "true" narrative—the Jewish/Israeli narrative—and that the Palestinian narrative is inherently flawed and dismissible. I believe that such thinking is wrongheaded and false, cruel and counter-productive. Such a posture will never address the problem between our two peoples, nor bring us closer to a peaceful resolution to the conflict.

The best strategy, and the one most likely to be effective, in my opinion, is that pro-Israel and pro-peace advocates (those who wish a two-state end-of-conflict agreement) speak, write, and otherwise transmit the truth always, acknowledging the legitimate positions of Israelis and Palestinians alike. The "truth" means affirming first that there are, indeed, two narratives—Israeli and Palestinian (I'll take this up more in the next letter); and second, that Israel has social problems and is an imperfect democracy relative to its national ideals expressed in its Declaration of Independence, and that holding onto the West Bank as occupiers will corrupt the soul of the people of Israel.

We have to acknowledge as well that there are anti-democratic trends growing within Israel that include the illegal, aggressive, and sometimes violent activities of some settlers vis à vis "mis-appropriation" (i.e., theft) of Palestinian-owned land and their relationship with neighboring Palestinians. We must recognize that the ultra-Orthodox political parties and rabbis hold a hostile approach to democracy and that middle-right Israeli political parties and their Diaspora Jewish supporters often acquiesce to extremist trends based on reasons of political self-interest.

Israel, like every other nation and western democracy in the world, is imperfect. Even Israel's most ardent defenders acknowledge this truth. We Jews ought not be defensive when legitimate criticism is leveled against the Jewish State. However, we have every right to challenge those who believe that Israel must behave according to a higher moral and legal standard than any other nation. That's not only unfair, but one has to suspect that something deeper is motivating the criticism. Those who challenge the right of the Jewish people to a state of our own but do not challenge the right of France, Italy, or Great Britain to that same right, are expressing not just anti-Zionism but anti-Semitism.

At the same time, it's important to note that there's a Jewish position that rejects Jewish nationalism. Many of those who take this position are ultra-Orthodox Jews who believe that the Jewish people can't create a state until the arrival of the Messiah. Others, such as the Jewish Voice for Peace, affirm Judaism's universal aspirations and reject political nationhood as an aberration in Jewish tradition and history. Some are non-Zionists and others are anti-Zionists. Just because these two groups do not accept Jewish nationalism, I don't believe they are necessarily anti-Semitic or self-hating Jews.

It would be easy for us living in America to disavow ourselves of the multi-pronged efforts to negate Israel's right to exist as the nation-state of the Jewish people. But we can't. Our self-respect as members of the Jewish people demands that we assert our own rights, not excluding ourselves from the same human rights we champion for others or rejecting the revolutionary step our people took in rewriting the narrative of victimhood to free ourselves in our own state.

Our rights and freedom need not, and should not, negate the rights of others. Daniel and David, I have faith that you will defend both. I know you have already done so, and that makes me one proud father.

ove,

Dad

Discussion Questions:

- The author discusses the Black Lives Matter Movement and Intersectionality. There is a vigorous debate taking place in the American Jewish community about whether American Jews ought to remain engaged with those groups and individuals with whom we share many values and liberal policy visions, but differ on our attitudes toward Israel in its relationship to the Palestinians. What do you think we American Jews ought to do—stay engaged and fight from within, or separate and oppose from the outside?

- Do you agree with the author's thoughts about when anti-Zionism is anti-Semitism? If not, why not?

- Do you believe that Israel was justified in building the security fence even though it causes hardship for Palestinians? Explain your position.

- The author notes that the Jewish Voice for Peace is concerned only with universal liberal values while rejecting Jewish tribalism and nationalism. Do you agree or disagree? Explain your position.

The Clash of Narratives and Rights

Dear Daniel and David,

Israelis and Palestinians each recount passionate histories of the multiple wars, terrorism, violence, and failed peace efforts they've imposed on each other and endured. Though the events chronicled are the same, each side has its own narrative featuring its own perspective of the conflict, its own explanation of who is right and wrong, why peace is elusive, which side is ready for peace and compromise, which is recalcitrant and maximalist in its thinking, and which is to blame for the failure to make peace on multiple occasions.

We tend to identify the good guys and the bad guys; when we look in the mirror we usually see ourselves in gleaming white hats.

But I'd like to urge that we step out of any fixed perspective we're accustomed to taking and get to know the history from both points of view. Only then can we see what each side might contribute to a solution and move forward optimistically. "Our problems are man-made—therefore, they can be solved by man," as President John F. Kennedy put it.[1] So too can the Israeli-Palestinian conflict be solved with visionary leadership if each side is willing to compromise and focus on the future instead of the past.

Part of the problem is that many Israelis and most Diaspora Jews don't know the Palestinian narrative, just as many Palestinians don't know the Israeli narrative. Many good-hearted people, Jews and non-Jews alike, have adopted uncritically a view that casts Israel as the oppressor of Palestinians and ascribe no responsibility to the Palestinians for perpetuating the conflict. A widespread lack of understanding and awareness of the truths of the *other* are among the obstacles to a pragmatic, secure, and comprehensive peace.

Why Peace and Truth Can't Live Together

To attain peace, both sides must set aside the idea that there's only one *Truth* and that they possess it. *Truth* (with a capital "T") that deals in absolutes and is unshaded by nuance is not conducive to the pursuit of peace. Such *Truth* is rigid and uncompromising. It insists that for one to win, the other must lose. It sees the world as black-and-white, all or nothing. Peace, by contrast, is yielding, malleable, and fluid. It accommodates and acknowledges shades of gray.

Peace seeks to understand the multiple truths of each side, working to discern the common ground between the poles. It's *both/and* not *either/or*. Complexity, humanity, and respect are essential in the peace narrative. So is compromise. The goal of peace is to leave both sides feeling they've won something of value and can emerge from conflict and negotiation with dignity and honor intact. Peace cannot come when one side belittles, demonizes, or obliterates the other. Peace results when each party feels understood, and each gives and gets. This is true between nations and peoples, and between individuals in marriage, families, friendships, and business.

Each Side Feels Victimized

At the center of the Israeli-Palestinian conflict is that each side claims the same land as its national home and regards the other as an adversary and themselves as victims.

For the Jewish people Israeli statehood is a phenomenon of historic magnitude. But for the Palestinians, the establishment of the State of Israel is a tragedy of epic proportions called "Nakba—The Catastrophe."

When large numbers of Jews began moving to Palestine in the early twentieth century, Palestinians began to feel that an invader was taking over their land. This is a primary reason Arab leadership never agreed to accept the partition of the land into an Arab and a Jewish state. They couldn't compromise their *Truth* and they went to war rather than accept compromise and peace. When Israel won the 1948 war and expanded its territory beyond the UN Partition plan lines, and then expanded again following the wars of 1967 and 1973, the Palestinians felt vanquished and victimized. They saw their homes destroyed, families separated, freedom and opportunities abridged.

Despite Israel's victory on the battlefield in all those wars that it believes were forced upon them by the Arabs, and despite its status as the most advanced nation in the Middle East with the most powerful army, Israel still regards the Palestinians as an ongoing threat and itself as a victim of terrorism.

Jewish Refugees from Arab Lands after 1948

Most people (Jews and non-Jews) don't know that 700,000 Jews who lived in Arab lands for centuries lost everything after Israel was established in 1948 and they were forced to flee their homes as anti-Semitism intensified. They were never compensated for their losses nor offered United Nations aid. Instead, Israel spent millions of dollars integrating them into Israeli life.

It's a tragedy that both sides are constrained by their narratives. Yet I have seen movement on the micro-interpersonal level that gives me hope that peace is yet possible. Person by person, group by group, Israelis and Palestinians can come to understand each other better, shift their entrenched attitudes and policies, restore justice, and weave a narrative of peace. It sounds impossible, but I've seen the impossible happen, and I want to share two examples of what it looks like.

When a Holocaust Survivor Confronts the Armenian High Priest

Daniel Rossing served for many years as Jerusalem's deputy mayor for religious affairs under Mayor Teddy Kollek, who was Mayor from 1965 to 1993. Daniel told my synagogue group a story that shows how Israeli Jews, despite Israel being the dominant power in the region and the majority population in the State of Israel, have a difficult time in their own minds letting go of their minority status and their identity as victims of anti-Semitism.

As Rossing tells the story, one Sunday afternoon in the mid-1970s following worship in the Church of the Holy Sepulchre, the Armenian Christian community, led by its high priest, walked in a joyful procession through the streets of the Old City to the Armenian patriarch's official residence near the Jewish quarter. The priest carried a large gold crucifix, and he clanged the base of it onto the pavement every few steps.

That day fell during the Jewish festival of Sukkot, and when the procession passed the apartment of a Jewish family with a Sukkah on its balcony, the woman who lived there was enraged by the sight and sound of the large crucifix so near her home. She picked up a pail of water and doused the high priest and his entourage.

To say the high priest was shocked, humiliated, demeaned, insulted, and furious is an understatement. He called Rossing at the Mayor's office and complained bitterly. Daniel went immediately to the patriarch's home and learned what had just taken place.

Daniel walked the narrow street to the Jewish woman's home, knocked on her door and introduced himself. He asked if he could have a few moments of her time. She welcomed him and listened as he described how gravely insulted the high priest had been when she threw water on his head.

She explained to Daniel that the sight of the crucifix in the priest's hands had reminded her of her childhood in Europe where she and her family were deported to Auschwitz while her Christian neighbors looked on passively and did nothing. She was the sole survivor in her large family.

"This is my home and this is my country. Those people are foreigners and my enemy," she proclaimed.

"Did you know that the high priest that you assaulted also regards Jerusalem as his religion's holy city and that he is the leader of the Jerusalem Armenian community?" Daniel replied. "He and his people too suffered starvation, deportation, mass murder, and genocide by the Turks in 1915. 1.5 million Armenians were murdered in a Holocaust of their own."

Stunned and embarrassed the woman said, "I didn't know that!"

Daniel returned to the high priest and told him the woman's story and his demeanor changed toward her as well.

Daniel arranged a meeting between the woman and the priest, who shared their stories and the meaning of Jerusalem in their lives. The Jewish woman apologized to the priest for her brazen insult. The priest accepted the apology with an open heart, and shared his compassion for the suffering she and her family had suffered.

From that day forward they lived side by side with empathy and mutual respect.

We soften one another's rigid narratives with our stories and our compassion.

When Israelis and Palestinians Meet at Hotel Everest

The second example takes place regularly in the town of Beit Jala, an Arab village between Jerusalem and Bethlehem, where Israeli Jews and Palestinian Arabs meet regularly at a local hotel to talk, learn about each other, promote empathy, grow in understanding, and share hopes for peace.[2]

A member of my synagogue community (Claudia Sobral) captured the possibilities of those interactions in a documentary film called "Hotel Everest" that focuses on the stories of two men who met there, 45-year-old Israeli soldier Eden Fuchs, and 50s-something Palestinian school director Ibrahim Issa. The men are unlikely friends.

Fuchs was a colonel in the Israeli Defense Forces who found his way to Hotel Everest after realizing that he had never personally known a Palestinian.

Issa was born in a refugee camp and had been shot by an Israeli soldier at a demonstration when he was 14, but grew to understand that violence is not the way to peace. He, too, wanted to understand the *other* and gravitated to discussions an American peace group was convening at the hotel.

The film follows the men as they co-lead the group's meetings and cope with the severe but everyday challenges of living among two peoples. Eden worries over sending his son into the army, where he'll be trained to see Ibrahim and his family as the enemy.

Ibrahim confined himself in his home as the Gaza war broke out in 2014; thousands of missiles were fired from his side of the border into Israel and Israel finally responded with a massive military campaign. During that war each man felt the pain of the other and feared for his friend because after years of sharing their stories with the community at Everest Hotel they had become dear friends.

The film records them over the course of two years and shows them, at one point, sitting together on a patio. "Eden has become my brother and I trust him with my life," Ibrahim says. Eden responds with obvious affection, smiles and says, "Thank you!"

We showed this film at my synagogue. Afterwards, we got to speak with both men. Eden was with us in the room and Ibrahim joined us from Bethlehem via Skype. I asked Ibrahim how he came to love and trust Eden, given their conflicting histories, experience, and national identities. It was that safe space at Hotel Everest, he replied, that opened his heart to compassion and friendship.

The film didn't address the politics of the Israeli-Palestinian conflict, but I couldn't resist asking each of the men what they believe to be the best political solution. They agreed that peace will be possible only when there's mutual respect and when each side acknowledges the dignity of the other. Peace can come, they said, when understanding removes ignorance, when compassion dispels hatred, and when Israelis and Palestinians meet as human beings and not as enemies.

Ibrahim said that he believed once in the two-state resolution of the conflict, but he now believes that the Jewish settlement enterprise throughout the West Bank has foreclosed a two-state solution. A one-state solution, he said, is the way forward—a state in which Palestinians and Israelis share equal rights and acknowledge the humanity of the other. I don't agree. Two states for two peoples is the only workable resolution to this conflict. For Jews who are far outnumbered in the region, a one-state solution would mean the end of the Zionist experiment, an end to our people's full independence, an end to Jewish self-determination, and the end of the Jewish State.

Israel and the Jewish people can't and shouldn't make that sacrifice. The 700,000 Jews in Arab lands who were forced to flee when Israel declared itself a state saw clearly their status in the Arab countries. Their welcome there was always conditional on their not possessing power. The same is true for all survivors of the Holocaust and immigrants who experienced anti-Semitism in its most brutal and demeaning formulation.

Having said this, I'm fully aware that Jewish sovereignty came at a terrible price for the 750,000 Palestinians who lost their place in the world even as we gained ours. I know and feel the injustice that continues as the occupation relentlessly compromises Palestinian rights and well-being. I believe the just solution to this untenable situation will give the Palestinians a democratic state of their own while Israel remains a separate state with a Jewish majority, steered by Jewish values and governed under democratic principles.

When a two-state resolution comes (I'm an eternal optimist, as you know), Jews will have to compensate Palestinians and give up land. Palestinians will have to agree to a secure peace. I would hope, as well, that the 700,000 Jews who fled Arab countries will also be compensated for their losses.

Being Pro-Israel Means Being Pro-Palestinian

I'm obviously pro-Israel, but being pro-Israel also means being pro-Palestinian. Peace can only be achieved with two states, and justice for the Palestinians is essential for a lasting peace.

Eden doesn't share my certainty. He told us that because he is neither a politician nor an expert in political science, he wouldn't express a political position. He believes that trust, respect, and compassion will result in the right political solution, whatever that may be. Even so, because of his compassion-building work with Ibrahim and the peace group behind the Everest Hotel project, Israeli Jewish extremists have accused him of being a traitor and of the "seed of Amalek."

Amalek is among the most vicious biblical enemies of the Israelites. Amalek and his minions attacked the elderly, women, and children from behind on the Israelites' flight from Egypt. Amalek became the Jewish symbol of evil. The villain Haman in the Esther story is said to be a descendent of Amalek, as well as Adolph Hitler and the Nazis. For Eden to be so accused is a serious and potentially deadly insult.

Given the volatile reality of violent nationalists within Israel, I asked Eden if he fears for his life. He says he isn't afraid, but that he often despairs about this unending conflict. He feels hopeful, he says, "when I reach out to my Palestinian peace partners and they accept my hand in friendship. I know that peace can come and my dreams are restored."

Ibrahim, too, has been accused of being a traitor. Palestinian extremists have denounced him for cooperating with Israel and contributing to the "normalization" of the occupation. But like Eden, he said he's unafraid and insists that the only way to peace is engagement with those with whom he disagrees.

I take heart in what Eden and Ibrahim and peace and human rights groups throughout Israel are doing. At great potential personal cost, they are showing us the way forward.

Perceiving the Same Events from Different Points of View

You can see the distance we have to bridge between our Israeli and Palestinian narratives of history in an excellent book called *Side by Side– Parallel Histories of Israel-Palestine*,[3] which was created by a group of Israeli and Palestinian educators after the second Palestinian Intifada (2000-2005). The book is filled with examples of the contrasting lenses through which each side views the same historical events, and it puts our differences in stark relief.

For instance, the Balfour Declaration of 1917, in which Great Britain noted that it "views with favour the establishment in Palestine of a national home for the Jewish People," is understood by Jews as a historic turning point, a major step toward a dream of statehood. For Palestinian Arabs, however, the Balfour Declaration was the beginning of a national disaster.

As the Palestinian contributors to *Side by Side* wrote:

> "…the establishment of the Zionist movement appeared as a radical international solution to the Jewish problem. Zionism embodied the transformation of Judaism as a religion into a nationalist bond which would be realized in a Jewish homeland and an exclusive Jewish state. A very important factor under which the Zionist movement was born, developed, and prospered was the increasingly competitive interests of the European world colonialist movement in Africa and Asia, and the Zionist movement's colonial interest in Palestine… The alliance of British imperialism and Zionism gave rise to what is known in history books as the Balfour Declaration on 2 November 1917."[4]

It's telling that even at this nascent stage, the going is exceedingly sticky, and each side can find itself trapped in *Truths* that are mutually exclusive, allowing neither room to compromise nor breathe.

The narrative at play in this passage equates Zionism with British imperialism and colonialism, and defines Jews in a way that we don't define ourselves. We have, for millennia, regarded ourselves as a people joined not only by religion, but by culture, traditions, ethics, law, language, and a history that connects us to Palestine, the Land of Israel. We are a people; and like every other people, we demand the right of self-definition. A narrative that reduces Judaism to a religion and erases all evidence to the contrary is disrespectful and offensive.

At the same time, there's truth in the Palestinian narrative. Our state has roots entwined with British imperialism; and yes, Jews and Palestinians were manipulated and betrayed by the British. History is always more complicated than calcified *Truth* suggests, and therein lies our hope for finding points of commonality and contact. We need the kinds of conversations that can come from comparing and responding to each other's experiences.

If we remain locked in our zero-sum narratives in which there's one winner in the contest for a home and sovereignty in this land, we'll never be able to find the peace we all want and so desperately need.

Dare to Hope

For a hopeful moment in 1988, Yasser Arafat and the PLO verbally accepted the existence of the State of Israel,[5] thus briefly opening the door to peace—although they didn't amend their Palestinian National Covenant to remove calls for Israel's destruction. At that moment we got a fleeting glimpse of possibility.

Since then, I've often been deeply pessimistic about our collective ability to set aside our entrenched suspicions and positions so we can construct a new narrative that respects our two peoples' rights and need for a home on this same parcel of land. Our habits are stubborn, our grievances generations old, our losses ever fresh. But then I witness the power of transformation between the Armenian high priest and a Holocaust survivor in Jerusalem, and between Eden and Ibrahim at the Hotel

Everest in Beit Jala, and I let myself hope that we can indeed build that new narrative together.

The distrust between the two sides, the conviction that the other side isn't willing to compromise its positions, the pain of the loss of loved ones on both sides—all make the possibilities for peace difficult to imagine.

New thinking is necessary. It likely will be up to your generation and future generations to work for a peaceful resolution to this seemingly intractable conflict. My Israeli friend Yaron Shavit likes to say "B'Yisrael ye-ush lo optsia—In Israel despair is not an option." We are, after all, a hopeful people.

Love,

Dad

Discussion Questions:

- Do you accept as legitimate the Palestinian narrative even as it is so different from the Israeli narrative? Does knowing the Palestinian narrative change how you regard the Israeli-Palestinian conflict?

- The author describes what is happening at Hotel Everest between Israelis and Palestinians who have entered into dialogue, and he notes that the two former enemies turned friends each did not want to speak about a political solution to the Israeli-Palestinian conflict. Instead, they each noted that attitudes can change when Israelis and Palestinians engage with each other and that whatever political solution emerges will be the right one. Do you agree?

- What political solution to the Israeli-Palestinian conflict do you think is best for Israelis and Palestinians and for the State of Israel—one democratic state in which Jews and Arabs are equal in every respect; one state that is not democratic but Jewish; two states for two peoples?

- Do you agree or disagree with the author's position that "being pro-Israel means being pro-Palestinian"?

Is There a Solution to the Israeli-Palestinian Conflict?

Dear Daniel and David,

The conflict between Israel and the Palestinians has been going on for 70 years, slightly longer than I've been alive. It's hard even for an optimist like me to believe that I'll live to see the day when a State of Israel and a State of Palestine live peaceably and cooperatively side by side. I hope that in your lifetimes you will see it.

To have peace, we have to be able to imagine it and work to create the conditions that might finally allow it to take root.

It's important to emphasize that although we live in the United States, we aren't bystanders to history; we're participants, no matter our role or where we live. Our individual visions contribute to a collective that has the power to hold the status quo in place or move in a new direction. I know you'll bring your own insights, passion, and wisdom to the process, and I'd like to share mine for you to consider and build upon.

I have no 10-point peace plan, no seat at a negotiating table. But after decades of observing the situation, spending time with thought leaders and ordinary people on both sides, and being part of the chorus of voices supporting the two-state solution, I've come to focus on four elements that have the power to move Israel and the Palestinians toward peace in their own independent states. I hope you will consider and support them as you carry on the work of helping to end this conflict.

Element 1: Bold and Visionary Leadership

It's been four decades since President Anwar Sadat of Egypt went to Jerusalem, spoke in the Knesset to the government of the Jewish State, and met with Israeli Prime Minister Menachem Begin and U.S. President Jimmy Carter at Camp David. The peace agreement that this trio of courageous leaders carved out between Egypt and Israel in 1977 still stands. Seventeen years later, Jordanian King Hussein and Israeli Prime

Minister Yitzhak Rabin met with President Bill Clinton to broker a peace agreement among their countries.

We've seen serious and noble attempts to bring the Palestinians and Israelis together to make peace. But the issues separating the two sides are in some cases seemingly irreconcilable and far more complex than those between Israel and Egypt, or between Israel and Jordan. It's our job to support groups and individuals who—like Sadat, Begin, Rabin, and Hussein—are willing to stand up to the polarized and intransigent forces that support entrenched *Truths* instead of peace. History has taught us how personally precarious it may be to take the lead with a radically moderate stance, and we owe our backing to those with the vision and courage to do so.

Element 2: Compromise

Compromise will be essential if a true peace is to occur. Each side will have to agree to accept less than it wishes if we're to see a future without violence. I know this is an obvious point, but it's a crucial one, which I've considered in detail in my letter on "The Clash of Narratives."[1] Compromise is central, too, in the approach to peace you'll see in Element 4, below.

Element 3: Asking Forgiveness on Both Sides

Israel and the Palestinians have inflicted great harm on one another, and there's no way to forge a peace agreement unless each side acknowledges its wrongs and asks forgiveness for them.

Daphna Golan-Agnon, an Israeli human rights and peace activist, has written movingly about her attempts to build trust with her Palestinian counterparts, and to break through the sense of denial, self-righteousness and unexpressed guilt that surrounds human rights violations, acts of terror and violence on both sides. In her book *Next Year in Jerusalem: Everyday Life in a Divided Land,* she recounts a meeting she had at an American conference at which participants discussed the Palestinian right of return. Suad, a Palestinian woman confided:

"I don't know what's wrong with me...I can't talk about this without my eyes filling with tears."

An Israeli asked: "What do you want, Suad? What do you want?"

Suad responded: "What do you think…can Israelis not say, 'we're sorry, we did you wrong,' because they're afraid that five million Palestinians will demand that they have the right of return to their homes in Israel?"

Golan-Agnon answered: "…I think it would be possible to persuade most Israelis to recognize the wrong done to the Palestinians if they were not afraid of the return of millions of Palestinians…Israel could say, 'We had no choice, but we're sorry for causing you so much pain when we established the state and expelled hundreds of thousands of people from their homes and lands, and then an international court could decide who among the Palestinian refugees is eligible to return to their own homes and lands, who returns to the future independent Palestinian state, who gets compensation, and who receives help settling in another country."[2]

Golan-Agnon, who is now a professor on the law faculty of the Hebrew University of Jerusalem, describes the way that Israel's history was explained to her in school in the 1960s. It was a narrative that pretended the lands that would become the Jewish State had been largely empty desert, and that the Arabs who did live there had little connection to the land.

"We were never told why the Palestinians were so angry with us," she writes. "We were never told what it was they wanted. I can't remember when I first understood that there were hundreds of thousands of Palestinians here before the establishment of the State of Israel."

Then she asks the question that I think is so central today: "Why is it so difficult for us to say we are sorry? We are sorry that we built a state for the Jews, who had been persecuted for so long, on your land, on land that Jews lived on centuries ago, to which we longed to return? We are sorry. Could we gather our courage to say such a thing—to apologize…."[3]

She and her children were born in Israel, and she doesn't advocate dissolving the nation that is her home or doing away with the Jewish State. But she makes clear that its future depends on acknowledging the damage that has been done to Palestine's Arabs and not perpetuating that damage by pretending away the experience of the other. Acknowledgment and apology work the other way too, I'll add. Palestinians have inflicted great pain on Israelis, and they too need to ask Israel for forgiveness.

The sad truth is that asking forgiveness of those we've wronged is among the most difficult challenges we ever face. We don't forgive easily for many reasons, including pride, self-righteous justification of what we did, and our lack of humility and empathy. Being unable to forgive is a sign of weakness in individuals and in nations. As Gandhi put it: "The weak can never forgive. Forgiveness is the attribute of the strong."[4]

Forgiving another doesn't mean that we pardon the one who hurt us. It means that we release the resentment we feel that keeps us from moving forward, unburdened by anger and rage. Forgiveness is a gift we give to ourselves. Golda Meir, a former Prime Minister of Israel said, "We can perhaps forgive the Arabs for killing our children, but we can never forgive them for forcing us to kill their children." We must reach for forgiveness, nonetheless.

We Americans know well the difficulty of moving our representatives to ask for forgiveness. It took 45 years for the American government to apologize formally to the 100,000 Japanese-American citizens it incarcerated in internment camps during World War II (Executive Order 9066). The Civil Liberties Act, which President Ronald Reagan signed in 1988, offered a formal apology to these loyal Americans and gave $20,000 to each surviving victim as compensation.[5]

It took more than a hundred years for the U.S. Congress to apologize to Native Americans "…for the many instances of violence, maltreatment, and neglect inflicted on Native Peoples by citizens of the United States." However, Congress offered no financial compensation.[6]

Not until 2008 did the U.S. House of Representatives offer a symbolic apology[7]—but no compensation—to the generations of African Americans who endured the horrors of slavery and subsequent Jim Crow laws that discriminated against them, holding them as second-class citizens in American society.

And the American government has yet to apologize to the people of Iraq for waging a destructive and stupid war that never should have been fought and cost the lives of over 100,000 Iraqi citizens.

Daniel and David—I remind you of all this to point out both the value of apology when it finally comes and the real difficulty of doing the right thing, even when there's broad, long-term recognition of injustice.

Reviewing these injustices in our own history gives us a chance to ask: What's fair? Are words enough? What conveys true forgiveness?

The Palestinians and Israelis each have much blood on their hands vis à vis the other, and their relentless conflict is deeply personal. As an individual, I would have a very hard time forgiving anyone who killed someone I loved, and so I appreciate how difficult it is for either nation to take that huge step—to apologize for the pain each inflicted on the other, and ask forgiveness. Perhaps the best we can expect are simple apologies from Israel's and the Palestinians' leaders. On the personal level, we can acknowledge the truths and pain of the other, along with the wrongs from which we have overtly or tacitly looked away. Peace is cumulative. It's passed from person to person.

A Moment of Hope

Many felt the power of an honest expression of mutual pain on September 13, 1993, when Prime Minister Yitzhak Rabin made remarks at the White House that acknowledged for the first time the suffering that both Israel and the Palestinians have endured at the hands of the other for so long. As I listened to Rabin, a former warrior, speak from the heart, I felt hopeful that peace actually could come to that troubled land. Here are some of his inspirational and courageous words that day in Washington, D.C.:

> We have come from a people, a home, a family that has not known a single year, not a single month in which mothers have not wept for their sons. We have come to try and put an end to the hostilities, so that our children, our children's children, will no longer experience the painful cost of war, violence and terror. We have come to secure their lives and to ease the sorrow and the painful memories of the past to hope and pray for peace.
>
> Let me say to you, the Palestinians: We are destined to live together on the same soil, in the same land. We, the soldiers who have returned from battle stained with blood, we who have seen our relatives and friends killed before our eyes, we

who have attended their funerals and cannot look into the eyes of their parents, we who have come from a land where parents bury their children, we who have fought against you the Palestinians.

We say to you today in a loud and a clear voice: Enough of blood and tears. Enough. We have no desire for revenge. We harbor no hatred towards you. We, like you, are people who want to build a home, to plant a tree, to love, to live side by side with you in dignity, in empathy, as human beings, as free [people]. We are today giving peace a chance, saying again to you: Enough. Let us pray that a day will come when we all will say: Farewell to the arms.

Element 4: Willingness to Negotiate the Easiest Terms First

Building on all this, I suggest to you a paradigm-shifting approach to peace that isn't original with me, though I wish it were because it's the smartest solution to the Israeli-Palestinian conflict that I've read anywhere. This plan:
- preserves Israel's democracy and Jewish character
- promises security for both Israel and a future Palestinian State
- enables the establishment of a demilitarized Palestinian state within definable borders
- allows a Palestinian capital in East Jerusalem
- deals with all concrete issues such as borders, water rights, work permits, and economic matters
- offers an opportunity for Israel to make peace with the moderate Arab and Muslim world
- normalizes relations with every other nation in the world that has been waiting for a resolution of this conflict

Utopia? Perhaps—but it's not as impossible as some might think.

At the heart of this approach proposed by Yossi Alpher, an Israeli security analyst and strategist, is the strategy of focusing on the issues that are most easily resolved, and setting aside the most contentious points of disagreement for a separate discussion.[8] That's a significant departure from the method that's been the template for negotiations to date: "Nothing is agreed until everything is agreed," which Alpher sees as a sure way to stay locked in an impasse.

Alpher brings significant experience to the analysis he lays out in detail in his 2016 book *No End of Conflict: Rethinking Israel-Palestine*. He was an officer in Israeli military intelligence and spent 12 years in the Mossad, Israel's secret service. He's been director of the Jaffee Center for Strategic Studies at Tel Aviv University. In July 2000 he served as a special adviser to the Prime Minister of Israel, Ehud Barak, during the Camp David peace talks led by President Bill Clinton. From 2001 to 2012 he and a former Palestinian Authority minister of planning co-edited a family of internet publications at bitterlemons.net, which housed a vigorous discussion of how best to bring peace to the region.

Alpher still believes that the only solution to the conflict is a negotiated two states for two peoples agreement that settles all issues. But after studying the Oslo process that set the course for all negotiations since, including the 2000 Camp David effort, the 2007 Olmert-Abbas secret negotiations, and the 2013-14 Kerry Initiative, Yossi concludes that further talks are doomed if they insist on first resolving the basic existential divide separating the two sides.

He quotes David Ben-Gurion's succinct definition of that core issue: "We, as a nation, want this country to be ours; the Arabs, as a nation, want this country to be theirs."[9] And then, in essence, he says, "So let's set that disagreement aside for a while and work to improve our lives in the meantime."

What a Two-Stage Negotiation Would Look Like

Alpher divides the issues that must be resolved into two groups. An intractable set of issues emerged after 1948: Israel's right to exist as a secure Jewish national home in Palestine, and Palestinian refugees' right to return to the land that was theirs before they fled or were removed after Israel declared statehood. These impassioned, irreconcilable national narratives must be shifted before progress can be made.

A separate, practical second set of issues arose after the 1967 Israeli-Arab War when Israel occupied the West Bank, the Old City of Jerusalem, East Jerusalem, and the Gaza Strip. On the Palestinian side, the priorities include establishing a Palestinian state with sovereignty, borders, a capital city in East Jerusalem, security, and the final disposition of Jewish settlements and Jews in a future State of Palestine.

On the Israeli side, priorities include establishing final international borders between the two states—roughly drawn along the Green Line—with land swaps to include the large settlement blocs in the State of Israel, thus assuring Israel's democracy and Jewish majority.

In all past negotiations, there has been much progress on the practical post-1967 issues. Alpher makes the case that negotiations henceforth ought to deal only with those. Should negotiations be successful on those issues, the Palestinians would achieve their state, sovereignty, national dignity, and security. Israel would achieve internationally recognized borders, maintain its Jewish and democratic character, and dramatically reduce the risks of violence and war. Israel would also likely be received more openly by moderate Arab and Muslim states in the region, and its western allies' relationships would be strengthened. The Boycott, Divestment, and Sanctions (BDS) movement's appeal would diminish dramatically, and the world Jewish community, now fractured, would rally as one to support Israel.

Palestinian Authority President Mahmud Abbas already agreed in his talks with former Israeli Prime Minister Ehud Olmert to demilitarize the future Palestinian state (except for a police force) and to allow Israeli and international combined forces to be stationed along the Jordan River for a period of time, the length of which is to be determined. Both leaders agreed that Jerusalem could become the capital city of both states.

Alpher insists that no more than this can be achieved at this time and that we continue with the status quo at our peril. I wholeheartedly agree.

His book will challenge you to think differently about this seemingly unending conflict and what might be necessary to address the many concrete, practical issues between Israel and the Palestinians before it's too late, and a one-state bi-national entity destroys Jewish and Zionist dreams.

The Settler Problem

There's a sense of urgency about moving negotiations forward because Jewish settlements continue to spread throughout the West Bank, making a future contiguous Palestinian state more difficult to achieve. Right-wing nationalist and messianic Israelis have taken over the Israeli government, and the Palestinian side, too, is succumbing to extremism. There's an ever-closing window that can accommodate a win-win compromise.

As recently as 2004, Prime Minister Ariel Sharon showed that Israel would be willing to withdraw Israeli troops from land the Palestinians claim as their own in Gaza.

There was virtually no violence between Jewish settlers and the Israel Defense Forces for two reasons. The first is that Gaza is not part of biblical Israel. Although Israeli settlers were deeply upset to be removed from their homes and businesses, which previous governments had promised would never be vacated, the area does not hold the same emotional attachment for Israel as does the West Bank (settlers call it by its Biblical names, Judea and Samaria). The Gaza evacuees were promised financial compensation and new homes elsewhere, although many have not been resettled all these years later.

The second reason there was no violence in the withdrawal is because the Israeli military handled the evacuation with great sensitivity.

But in that peaceful move, the groundwork was laid for deep suspicion. Today's Israeli settlers not only mistrust government promises to resettle them in the large settlement blocs or on the Israeli side of the security fence, they also mistrust the Palestinians. When Israelis withdrew from their Gaza farms, they left their highly developed businesses behind and the Gazans destroyed everything. If that wasn't enough to sour Israelis toward the Palestinians, once Hamas took over the Gaza Strip in a military coup against its own Palestinian Authority in 2007, anti-Israel rejectionists fired thousands of missiles indiscriminately at Israel and provoked two wars within five years (2009 and 2014).

Many Israelis now will refuse to withdraw from any territory in the West Bank—not only because they consider the West Bank to be part of greater Israel as stated in the Hebrew Bible, but also out of fear that Hamas will stage another coup against the Palestinian Authority and take over the entire Palestinian government, thereby posing a mortal threat to Israel.

A word about annexation of the large settlement blocks before a negotiated solution is achieved. Prime Minister Netanyahu promised to do this in the first 2019 election campaign, a campaign that did not ultimately succeed in forming a ruling government coalition. For Israel to change the status quo before talks resume and agreement is reached on the 1967 issues is an enormous mistake. Already, the Palestinian Authority (PA) is weak and political pundits in Israel and the United States worry that the PA will not continue to survive as a representative body for the more moderate Palestinians it represents. Any unilateral move by Israel will bring about the death of the PA. As weak as it is already, having no representative body on the Palestinian side with which to negotiate will not augur well for a future negotiated settlement.

It is my hope that any future Israeli government will not attempt unilaterally to change the status quo.

Is There Flexibility Among Palestinians for a Two-State Solution?

The short answer is yes, but it is more complicated than that.

Two surveys by Palestinian pollsters taken in October 2018 show "unexpected popular flexibility on core issues of an eventual peace deal with Israel, despite widespread skepticism among Palestinians about current prospects." David Pollock, writing as the Bernstein Fellow at The Washington Institute[10] reported that two-thirds of Gazans say Palestinians should accept the "right of return" only to the West Bank and Gaza, and not Israel. Only 14 percent say they would "probably" move to Israel if they could. On the topic of "permanent resettlement," 79 percent say they would accept Palestinians from other countries in the West Bank or Gaza only. And 59 percent want Arab states to provide financial assistance to resettle Palestinian refugees in the West Bank or Gaza, but not in Israel.

In the West Bank a solid majority think that "regardless of what's right, the reality is that…most Palestinians will not return to the lands they vacated in 1948."

The survey showed that if Israel "recognizes an independent Palestinian state and ends the occupation of the West Bank and Gaza, 55 percent of

Gazans, 36 percent of West Bank residents, and 60 percent of residents in East Jerusalem would accept Israel as 'the state for the Jewish people.'"

It's important to keep in mind that the leadership of the Palestinian Authority and Hamas are at odds with their own people and say they will never agree to what Gazans and West Bank Palestinians are prepared to accept.

Of West Bank Palestinians polled, 50 percent agree to the concept of a two-state solution, as opposed to 37 percent who insist on liberating all of Palestine. In Gaza, the split is 47 percent for a two-state solution and 49 percent for all of Palestine. In East Jerusalem, the margin is 73 percent for a two-state solution as opposed to 22 percent for all of Palestine.

One of the two polls showed that the majority of Gazans favor Israel's destruction, whereas 30 percent of West Bank Palestinians favor Israel's destruction and 58 percent oppose it. In East Jerusalem, 36 percent of Palestinians favor peace with Israel, 47 percent oppose it, and 17 percent refused to answer the question.

The surveys suggest that popular Palestinian opinion is less harsh toward Israel as a Jewish state than is the leadership of the PA and Hamas.

What About the Israeli Side?

On the Israeli side, given the Palestinian Authority and Hamas leaderships' unwillingness to entertain compromise, the possibility of Israeli withdrawal from the West Bank is difficult to imagine even should there be a peace treaty.

Many Israeli residents of small West Bank communities might be willing to move back across the Green Line and into Israel itself or into the larger settlement blocs that likely will remain in Israel in a peace agreement, with the condition that they be adequately compensated and homes found for them. However, there's a small but not insignificant group of ideologically driven extremist settlers, perhaps 10 percent of the settler population (25,000-50,000 Jews) that would violently resist their own government's decision. I worry that such a powder keg would explode into a civil war with many Jews dead at the hands of other Jews, and a deepening polarization in the Israeli population and the Jewish world.

In the end, what Israel does only Israelis can decide; for they are the ones who must live with the direct consequences of their decisions. That being said, we Diaspora Jews have a deep interest in what Israel does, and we can support the country's voices of moderation and encourage the forces working to rein in the extremist minority.

None of this, discouraging as it is, should stand in the way of vigorous attempts to broker the sort of deal Yossi Alpher suggests. For so many friends of Israel, the excruciating choice is to trust and wait for the right time to make peace (which may never come) or to make peace and trust that hostilities will abate. I go for the latter. Alpher's analysis and prescription for peace and security is a way forward.

Love,
Dad

Discussion Questions:

- The author cites Yossi Alpher's proposal, which separates 1948 issues from 1967 issues. Alpher recommends dealing only with issues from 1967, and leaving the 1948 issues for the next generation to solve. Do you agree with his approach or disagree?

- What do you think the future holds for Israel and the Palestinians, given the current hostilities between the two peoples?

- What are the greatest challenges for Israel and the Palestinians in finding a peaceful and negotiated resolution of their conflict?

- The two surveys David Pollock cites show that popular Palestinian opinion is more flexible than the attitudes of the leadership of the Palestinian Authority and Hamas. Does that give you hope that Alpher's program or an end-of-conflict resolution of the Israeli-Palestinian conflict is possible?

Why Jerusalem is Not a Unified City

Dear Daniel and David,

We've been to Jerusalem together many times, and I think you'll agree with me that Jerusalem is a wondrous city: ancient and modern, and a metaphor for everything happening in Israel in its relationships with its neighbors and the Christian and Muslim worlds. In real terms and as metaphor, Jerusalem straddles the fault lines of every possible conflict in the region.

Stand on the roof of the Church of the Holy Sepulchre, as I've done a number of times, and you'll have a magnificent, 360-degree view of synagogues, churches, mosques, and buildings raised by a parade of nations. As you know, the city is relatively a small place, but that piece of holy real estate occupies the imagination of billions of people around the world.

In its long history, Jerusalem (meaning "City of Peace") has rarely been without conflict. It's been attacked 52 times, captured and recaptured 44 times, besieged 23 times, and destroyed twice. What happens there is monumentally important, and those who love and care about Israel have to tread carefully—especially since Israel controls this holy city. Negotiations on the issues of access to holy sites and shared use of the ancient spaces are delicate, and always seem to be one tiny spark away from incendiary.

Talking about the city today inevitably takes us back centuries into some of the most important stories of Judaism, Islam, and Christianity, many of which converge on this site. Within each of those traditions, it's important to remember that there are fundamentalists who take literally the stories told in their holy literature, as well as those who regard those stories symbolically. The battles over what's significant and what's appropriate use of the space are not only cross-cultural, they are also complicated by interpretation on all sides.

Our tradition places our people in the city beginning around the year 1200 BCE, as described in the Biblical books of Joshua and Judges. King

David, our stories tell us, arrived around the year 1000 BCE, ushering in a new era of Jewish history. He was among the first to recognize the religious and strategic importance of the city. The Torah describes how he brought the Ark of the Covenant (Exodus 25) containing the stone tablets inscribed with the 10 Commandments to the City of David, located just south of today's Old City walls over a spring of water, which is why David established his reign there. Already a city in pre-Davidic times, Jerusalem became the capital city of his kingdom.

David was followed as king by his son Solomon, who began his reign around 950 BCE. He expanded alliances dramatically (legend says he had 1,000 wives, all of whom cemented the kingdom behind his rule in relationship to a multiplicity of tribes in the surrounding area), and built the first Temple of Jerusalem, which most likely housed the Tabernacle (i.e., the Ark of the Covenant) that David had placed in the "City of David" just down the valley.

In the following centuries, the city was conquered by a who's who of regional, international, and religious powers: Assyrians, Babylonians, Persians, Greeks, Romans, Muslim Califs, Christian Crusaders, and the Muslim leader Saladin. By the eleventh century, Christian rulers had returned. They were displaced by the Ottomans in the fifteenth century and then, in the twentieth century, by the British; and then by Israel and the Hashemite Kingdom of Jordan, each of which controlled half of the city. After the 1948 War of Independence, Jordan controlled East Jerusalem and the Old City, and Israel controlled West Jerusalem. In 1967, Israel fought and won the Arab-Israeli War and took control of East Jerusalem and the Old City.

A City of Multiple and Interlocking Faith Traditions

At issue in today's Jerusalem are ancient buildings that anchor the beliefs of Jews, Muslims, and Christians—and sometimes lie almost literally on top of one another. Key is the Temple Mount, the site where the first Temple of Jerusalem stood for four centuries, and where Jewish Midrashim (legends) say Abraham was prepared to sacrifice his son Isaac (Genesis 21).

The Temple was destroyed by the Babylonian King Nebuchadnezzar in the sixth century BCE, and rebuilt in 20-19 BCE by Herod, a Judean whom the Romans installed as king. Herod, a master builder, had the new Temple of Jerusalem constructed on a massive platform that spreads across the equivalent of 36 acres that is still there. Excavations at the base of the retaining wall on the western side of the platform reveal two huge boulders, each weighing five tons, perfectly placed on top of each other. How the ancient engineers accomplished such feats is a mystery.

That Temple was gone less than a century later, destroyed in 70 CE by the Roman general Titus, an event recorded in a relief carved for a victory arch near the Forum in Rome.[1] That's an important detail because millennia later, there's political contention over whether that Temple or its predecessor ever existed, and how important they were to Jewish life. The relief, showing a Jew carrying on his back the Temple's seven-branched menorah (described in Exodus 25) after the Roman attack, is concrete proof.

Another piece of evidence: archaeologists uncovered very near the southern steps outside the platform leading up to the Temple compound ancient ritual baths described in the Talmud (Eruvin 4b and Yoma 31a) that were used by Jewish pilgrims before they ascended to the Temple to offer sacrifices.

Christianity's Church of the Holy Sepulchre and Islam's Noble Sanctuary

Within walking distance of the Temple compound is the site (in its time outside the city walls) where Christians believe Jesus was executed on the cross (circa 30 CE) by Pontius Pilate, the Roman governor of Judea. The Church of the Holy Sepulchre was built over this spot in the third century CE.

Muslims, for their part, believe that Mohammed (b. 570 CE) took a miraculous journey from Mecca to Jerusalem in one night and ascended to heaven from a stone located at the precise place where the second Temple once stood. On this night, understood as both miracle and dream, Mohammed is said to have met the earlier prophets including Abraham, Moses, and Jesus, and received instruction from God for his people. In the seventh century CE, the rock from which Muhammed is said to have ascended was enshrined in a structure called the Dome of the Rock. Built in 691 CE, the original dome collapsed three centuries later in 1015 CE. It was rebuilt seven years later and stands today as among the most magnificent and oldest works of Islamic art and architecture in the world.

Muslim tradition relates that Mohammed tethered his donkey, Buraq, to the Western Wall (the Jewish "Wailing Wall"—the retaining wall of the Temple compound) before visiting God. In Islam, that site is called the "Wall of Buraq."

Because of the sacred importance of these holy sites to the three great world religions, Israel has particularly cared for the maintenance of and protection of these sites since 1967—when the State of Israel took control of the Old City. But these sites have not always been treated with sensitivity, particularly in wartime. During the fighting in the 1948 War, when Jordan governed the West Bank, the Old City of Jerusalem and East Jerusalem, Jordanian troops blew up the Old City's ancient synagogues and later desecrated the Mount of Olives' ancient Jewish cemetery, using its ancient tombstones with Hebrew inscriptions to build roads and Jordanian army latrines.

The 1967 War transferred control of Jerusalem to Israel, but the new government didn't permit Jews to pray on the Temple Mount. Rabbis were concerned that Jews might inadvertently step on and thereby desecrate the holy site that was permitted only to the High Priest on one day of the year (Yom Kippur), and the new government wanted to keep peace with the Muslim Waqf, a trust which controlled the Noble Sanctuary that sits on the ancient Temple site.

MK Yehuda Glick: "The Most Dangerous Jew in Israel"

Jews still avoid praying anywhere on the platform surrounding the Dome of the Rock for those reasons. There is now, however, a small group of Jews in a coalition called HaLiba that is dedicated to "reaching complete and comprehensive freedom and civil rights for Jews on the Temple Mount." It is led by Member of the Knesset Yehuda Glick, with whom I have personally become friendly.

Yehuda is an Orthodox American immigrant living on a settlement in the West Bank who supports a one-state solution to the Israeli-Palestinian conflict. He believes that Arabs and Jews in Israel ought to be equal in every respect: enjoying the same rights including the right to vote, to be a part of the Israeli government, and even if it were to come to pass, to serve as Prime Minister of Israel. There we disagree; you know how strongly I support the two-state solution.

Yehuda believes as well that Reform and Conservative Jews and Women of the Wall have the right to their own prayer space at the Western Wall to the immediate south of the traditional prayer site beneath Robinson's Arch. He believes that we non-Orthodox Jews ought to be able to control our prayer space and prayer practices free from the supervision and intrusion of the ultra-Orthodox administrator of the Wall. I too hope that will come to pass.

Most strikingly, he supports the incendiary idea of building a synagogue on the Temple Mount, which would set off a religious conflagration on a site that now maintains a delicate peace. He believes that Jerusalem is different than any other city on the planet. It is the "City of Peace" and that means that all peoples, regardless of their religious preferences, should have the right to pray as they choose without interference from anyone. He wants a synagogue built alongside the Dome of the Rock and the Al Aqsa Mosque on the large 36-acre platform. I strongly object to this ever happening and told Yehuda that he risked sparking World War III with Muslims should he ever succeed.

Any attempt to change the status quo on that platform is forbidden by the Muslims and Israeli authorities. Consequently, Yehuda's activism has resulted in his being arrested dozens of times as he attempted to ascend to the Temple Mount to organize Jewish prayer services. He has been called the most dangerous man in Israel because should he ever succeed in establishing a synagogue there, we could expect a Muslim holy war that engulfs the Muslim world of more than one billion people and is aimed at Israel.

Yehuda isn't stupid. To the contrary, he is exceptionally bright and he understands all of this. He assured me that reaching his goal will not come soon. "It will take much time and will require many baby steps," but he believes that it is coming. He isn't in a hurry. He urges everyone to be as tolerant and accepting of the other as possible. I was surprised to like him, even as his militant talk of peace incites violence—including an attempt on his life four years ago that he survived.

Yehuda is a good man. But in Israel (and especially in Jerusalem today), the way to peace doesn't involve occupying more territory—especially the most sacred site of another religion—regardless of our own past history on that site. Good, smart men can also be very wrong and Yehuda is very wrong indeed!

A Lot of Motion and Very Little Movement

The challenge before Israel is to maintain the status quo among the religions of Jerusalem. Daniel Rossing, who I mentioned earlier in the story about the Holocaust survivor and the Armenian high priest, explained just how difficult that is. As he walked through the city with my synagogue group and me, he pointed out a ladder (called the "status quo ladder") that was leaning against a window on a balcony above the main portico of the Church of the Holy Sepulchre. This ladder was first mentioned in 1757 and it has remained in that exact location since then, except for being temporarily moved on two occasions.

The ladder cannot be moved because of an understanding that says no cleric of the six ecumenical Christian orders of the church may move, rearrange, or alter any property without the consent of the other five orders. That means the Latins (Roman Catholics), Greek Orthodox, Armenian, Syriac Orthodox, Coptic Christians, and Ethiopian Christians must all agree—and consensus can take centuries, if it ever comes. Keep in mind that this is an internal Christian matter and they don't have the core differences that come with being Jewish or Muslim.

Rossing told us several stories about the church. One that is particularly amusing and revealing concerns a small chapel in the larger church that's used by two of the six religious orders. This chapel, small and with a dirt floor, is lit by a single light bulb hanging from a wire attached to the ceiling.

One night around 11:00, Daniel received an urgent phone call from one of the high priests who had rights to the use of this chapel: "Daniel—there is a serious problem in the chapel. I have a service scheduled for 7:00 a.m. and the light bulb has gone out!"

"Let me investigate and I'll get back to you," Daniel told him.

Soon after, another urgent call came to Daniel from the high priest of the other order that had rights to the chapel, and he said essentially the same thing: "Daniel—I have a serious problem because I have a service scheduled for 8:00 a.m. in the chapel and the light bulb has gone out."

"Let me investigate and I'll get back to you," Daniel repeated reassuringly.

Daniel got dressed, called Adeeb Joudeh, a Muslim whose family for centuries has possessed the key to the church as a sacred trust. Daniel explained the situation to Adeeb and they met near midnight at the Jaffa Gate to the Old City. They walked together to the church. Adeeb opened the door and Daniel went directly to the chapel and changed the bulb. He thanked Adeeb, returned home and went to bed.

Daniel deliberately awoke early and called the first high priest at 5:00 a.m., waking him up. Daniel used an angry voice and said: "I'm very upset with you. You got me out of bed in the middle of the night. I called Adeeb to meet me at Jaffa Gate. We walked to the church and he graciously opened the door for me. I went to the chapel to investigate your claim that the bulb was out and I found that the light bulb was just fine. Please don't call me for such trivial things again without checking for yourself whether what you heard is true!"

Daniel called the other high priest and told him the same thing.

Each priest apologized profusely and thanked Daniel for his and Adeeb's efforts.

Of course, this was a big game, but a game that was played because of the agreement among the orders not to make any material change without everyone else's okay—even if it meant changing a light bulb or moving a ladder. They needed Daniel, a trusted mediator and a stealth actor in a drama involving two high priests, and Adeeb to make the game work.

"That's the Middle East," Daniel explained to us. "Everything here hangs in a delicate balance, and when the status quo is disturbed, violence can result."

An Israeli scholar explained to me once that in the Middle East "there's always a lot of motion but very little movement," and I've found that to be more profound than it may seem.

The city of Jerusalem specifically and the Middle East generally are made up of many competing interests and ancient cultures, and so a tacit understanding evolved that accepts change very slowly. Perhaps this is one of the reasons that the establishment of the State of Israel was such a traumatic event to so many in the Middle East. Israel's birth was far more than motion. It was a giant movement and, recalling Isaac Newton's Third Law of Physics, there has been for 70 years "an equal and opposite reaction."

On a recent trip to Israel, I took my congregants again to the Church of the Holy Sepulchre. There we encountered a group of about 30 brightly clad Christian pilgrims from Ghana who were unaware of the Church rule that no service could be conducted without the approval of all the clerics of the six religious orders. These people prayed in tongues just outside the tomb inside the Church. It was fortunate that there wasn't a major incident. Fights have broken out for reasons far less significant.

I present Jerusalem this way because I want you to know not only how key Jerusalem is to the identity of all three religious traditions, but also because these stories reveal how complicated the Middle East is as a whole.

Not a Unified City

Since the 1967 War, Israel has controlled all of Jerusalem, and it has built massively to create a number of Jewish neighborhoods in a ring around the city, thus expanding the city limits. Every Israeli government proclaims that Jerusalem will never be divided again, that it is one city and will remain in Israeli hands.

Of course, the city is not really unified. There's West Jerusalem, which is Israeli Jewish, and East Jerusalem, which is primarily Palestinian Muslim, plus the Old City that's divided into four parts, like the four chambers of the heart: a Jewish quarter, an Armenian quarter, a Christian quarter, and a Muslim quarter.

East Jerusalem has almost nothing to do with West Jerusalem. Though Palestinians are given the right to vote in municipal elections, they can't vote in national elections because they aren't citizens of the State of Israel. Further, out of fear of violating the principle of "cooperating with the occupation," few Palestinian Arabs vote in municipal elections, nor do they run for city council. They risk a death sentence by extremist Palestinians if they do.

Because East Jerusalem Palestinian Arabs don't hold office and vote, they have little or no influence on what takes place in their own neighborhoods. Frustration begets violence begets frustration in a seemingly never-ending cycle. After the Knife Intifada, checkpoints were set up throughout the eastern segment, making travel difficult.

Silwan, a neighborhood just south of the City of David, is a disturbing example of further extremist Jewish anti-Arab aggression. The area is primarily a Muslim Palestinian neighborhood, but a group called Elad, ultra-Orthodox Jews in charge of the excavation of the ancient city where David reigned as King 3,000 years ago, is attempting to buy property and assert its right to populate the village which was once the home of many Jews. On the surface, such efforts might not seem abnormal. But given the context of tension and hostility between the Jewish and Palestinian populations, the Jewish settlers often act with impunity, bullying their way in.

City services aren't allocated equally between Jerusalem's Jewish and Palestinian Arab neighborhoods. Prime Minister Benjamin Netanyahu and President Reuven Rivlin have made a commitment, to their credit, to change this and allocate equal shekels to each sector, but the changes are slow in coming.

Should there be a Palestinian State, a principal Palestinian demand is to locate their capital somewhere in East Jerusalem. Where their government buildings would be is a big question. For Israel to go forward and agree to the establishment of a Palestinian State (as I hope it will one day do) without Jerusalem as its capital is a non-starter. It's my view that this demand must be met for there to be peace.

There was a time when a majority of Israelis agreed to a Palestinian capital in Jerusalem in a two-states for two peoples resolution of the conflict; but as time passes, that has become a minority opinion.

Since President Trump's recognition of Jerusalem as the capital of Israel and commitment to build the American Embassy there, Palestinian Authority leadership reacted negatively and refused to accept American mediation by President Trump in eventual restored peace talks with Israel. Trump countered by saying that by recognizing Jerusalem as Israel's capital, the most difficult negotiating issue has been removed. His attitudes reveal a profound ignorance of the dynamics and a total lack of sensitivity to the nature of the tensions between Israel and the Palestinians.

Jerusalem is a central issue for both Israelis and the Palestinians. Had President Trump said, when recognizing Jerusalem as Israel's capital, that he also looked forward one day to East Jerusalem being the capital of a future Palestinian state, the Palestinians might have been supportive of his statement.

During the Knife Intifada of 2015-2016 (also known as the "Wave of Terror," "Intifada of the Individuals," or "Stabbing Intifada"), I visited an all-girls Palestinian Muslim middle school and high school in East Jerusalem and met with eighth-grade students. One of their schoolmates was being held in isolation by Israeli police at Hadassah Hospital in West Jerusalem for injuries she sustained when she attacked Israeli soldiers with a kitchen knife. The entire school was on her side, claiming that she was innocent of attacking Israelis, and that she was arrested for no reason. Her schoolmates demanded that she be released from the hospital to the custody of her parents.

This incident revealed to me how very different are the perceptions and narratives of the Israeli Jewish and Palestinian Muslim populations in Jerusalem, and how fraught with tension and hostility are the relationships.

In my conversation with these students, they told me that they have almost no contact with Israelis, except Israeli soldiers. They confessed that they neither like nor trust Israeli Jews and were surprised to learn that I'm a rabbi. "You don't look like a rabbi!" they said, thinking of black-hat Haredi rabbis. They were touched that my group of rabbis from the United States had come to visit, that we were interested in them and expressed concern for their situation.

Though Israel is responsible for security for all of Jerusalem and is committed to bringing more civic services to the Arab sectors, it's a mistake to claim that Jerusalem is in any other way unified. East Jerusalem Palestinians work in Israeli hotels and that's a point of contact, but there's little to commend the idea of unity in the real world. Perhaps there is such unity in the minds and vision of the people of Israel, but such unity doesn't exist in the hearts of the people. Until it does, there can't be peace. It will be necessary for both Israeli Jews and Palestinian Arabs to have more personal contact with each other, to hear from each other their stories, and then hopefully to develop greater understanding, compassion, and empathy.

The image of the old city of Jerusalem as a beating heart with four chambers is apt. It is a metaphor for what could be—a unified Jerusalem in which each quarter represents Jerusalem and, more widely, Israel. A heart that beats as one, that is dependent for its well-being on the well-being of each quarter. That's something I hope you and your generation will understand and help support in any way you can.

Love,

Dad

Discussion Questions:

- Which of the following positions do you most believe is reasonable, realistic, and in Israel's and the Palestinians' best interest?

  ¨ a unified city under Israeli security control with equal resources given to Jewish and Palestinian Arab sectors

  ¨ a city that houses both the Jewish and Palestinian capitals of their states but remains unified under Israeli security control with Palestinian police in the Arab sector

  ¨ a divided city controlled by Israel on the Israeli side and Palestine under control by the Palestinians on the Palestinian side

  ¨ a unified city under the control of an international body such as the United Nations, the United States, the Arab League, NATO, or the European Union

  ¨ Critique each of the above options and then consider what political solution is pragmatically in the best interest of all the inhabitants and groups within the larger Jerusalem municipality.

- The author tells the story of Member of the Knesset Yehuda Glick, who wants to set up a synagogue on the Temple Mount/ Haram al Sharif, and for Jerusalem to be a city of true peace between all peoples. Do you agree that he is the "Most dangerous Jew in Israel?" If so, why? If not, why not?

Why Hebrew Matters

Dear Daniel and David,

One of the marvels of Israel is the way it turned ancient Hebrew into a living, working language. Hebrew helped to unify a diverse collection of Jews from around the world and build a dynamic, forward-facing culture.

To understand not just Israeli politics but the wealth of innovation, artistry, and tech leadership that's emerging from the Jewish state and the minds of your Israeli cousins, you'll need to speak their language. As never before, it makes sense to learn Hebrew.

I've been studying Hebrew on and off since I was 21 years old, and I count it as one of the most important things I've done in my adult life. I'm happy to be able to speak and understand much of what I hear when Israelis talk to me, though I don't know Hebrew slang and many colloquialisms. I suspect that I'll continue my studies and struggles with the language for the rest of my days.

Hebrew, as you might know, is ranked by linguists as among the most difficult languages in the world to learn as a second language. However, that shouldn't stop you from trying to enhance your Hebrew knowledge. If you need to, take it a word or phrase or verse or idea at a time. I just spent an enjoyable couple of minutes reviewing vocabulary with Mango Languages, which is offered free online through our local library. The options are many—and the time you invest in language practice is worth it. Learning Hebrew will change your life and open a door to Judaism and the Jewish people that you can't reach in any other way. Yes, you can read much in translation; but to use a vivid image, doing that is like making love with your clothes on. It just isn't as good. Translations are never exact, and they miss cultural references and associations. They are essentially commentary, and every translator has a unique perspective to advance. It's far preferable to go straight to the source.

The truth is that most American Jews don't know Hebrew. About half of them can't read the Hebrew aleph bet, and only about 15 percent can follow a basic conversation or read an easy sentence. Only four percent are Hebrew speakers. That means that we are keeping ourselves at arm's length from any real possibility of communicating with Israelis despite the fact that so many Israelis speak English. My most satisfying time in Israel is when I encounter non-English speakers and our common language is Hebrew.

David Hazony, an American-born Israeli journalist and translator who now heads The Israel Innovation Fund, makes the tough-love case that "American Jews have much to contribute to Hebrew discourse and our collective Jewish future. Their tradition of tolerance and religious liberalism, their democratic experience and their philanthropic habits, to name just a few things. But they will do so only if they dispense with the ignorance-as-wisdom arrogance that locks them out of Hebrew-based culture." [1]

Ahad Ha'am, the founder of cultural Zionism, wondered what a Jewish nation would produce in a setting where "its spirit will find pure expression and develop in all its aspects up to the highest degree..." [2] What we've been seeing in recent years from Israelis is just how rich and multi-faceted their free-spirited, Hebrew-based culture has become. They've produced, among many other innovations, business concepts like WeWork and Wix; lifesaving strategies for bringing clean water to a world that's drying up; the pure cultural deliciousness of Yotam Ottolenghi; the breakthrough thinking of Daniel Kahneman and Amos Tversky, whose collaboration Michael Lewis documented in *The Undoing Project*; the wonder of Gal Gadot and TV shows like "Homeland" and "In Treatment." As Hazony and Adam Scott Bellos noted in *The Jerusalem Post*, "Zionism has always been about the Jews channeling the power of their creative-moral intellect into every facet of human life." And this is what happens when they do. [3]

It's a creativity honed from resilience and innovation, born of life under pressure and fashioned from layers of influences from around the world that have been melded with Hebrew. *This*, not war, is Israel's essence—exciting as any culture anywhere in the world. And Hebrew can unlock it for you. Hebrew is the way into the Jewish soul: the language of prayer, Torah, philosophy, mysticism, literature, Zionism, and the direct experience of what is being created and lived in Israel today.

It will take work to be able to enter the conversation in its native language, but as Hazony has said, "without fluency in Hebrew, the engagement with Israeliness will always be a dilution and distortion based on intermediaries looking to explain things for Americans rather than the immersive, direct exposure that a personal journey requires. Only the language carries the nuance, the instinct, and, ironically, all that is unsaid."[4]

The best way to learn is to go to Israel and study on Ulpan, an intensive Hebrew immersion course. There are many Ulpanim (plural for Ulpan) available. If you can afford it, I highly recommend Ulpan Or in Jerusalem or Tel Aviv. I've studied in Jerusalem and with teachers in both cities from Los Angeles by Skype. One-on-one learning will enable you to progress far more rapidly than learning in a room full of others with different language capacities.

There are many levels of Hebrew competence, and anything is better than nothing. The first and most basic level is to be able to recognize Hebrew letters, read words, and follow along in religious services.

The second is to be able to comprehend what you read, to be able to pick out words and know what they mean.

The third is to be able to converse using simple language.

The next is more advanced speaking and comprehension.

Then there's reading and listening to the news. *The Jerusalem Post* publishes a simple edition in Hebrew with vowels. Articles cover current events, holidays, and culture. The paper provides vocabulary with punctuation and definitions so you don't have to look through a dictionary. There are now apps, by the way, that can translate from Hebrew to English and English to Hebrew quickly.

The highest level, of course, is speaking and reading fluently—but that takes time and concentrated effort.

Biblical Hebrew is different than Modern Hebrew, and I recommend that you focus on the language you can use in conversation today.

Modern Hebrew has developed dramatically over time. I have at home three Hebrew biographies of my great-great Uncle Avraham Shapira. I tried my hand once at translating one of these books. It was difficult because the Hebrew was written in the 1930s and 1940s, and many words are no longer used or have evolved to have new meanings.

A newly published book called *The Story of Hebrew* by Lewis Glinert[5] describes how the language developed through the millennia. I was fascinated to see how it was resurrected first as a literary language beginning in the eighteenth century, and then as a spoken language beginning in the early twentieth century. It still astonishes me that it is now the official language of an entire nation.

Daniel and David, each of you has learned some Hebrew. If you have an opportunity to study it again, I hope you will do so. I hope it will lead you into real-life conversations with people who can share the best of what's happening in Israel today, as well as into discussions about the issues that are most important to you. You have enough knowledge already to pick up where you left off and enjoy throwing yourselves into the language again.

A poem written years ago by Danny Siegel, called simply "Hebrew," expresses how I feel about this remarkable language of the Jewish people. I hope some of that feeling rubs off on you!

Hebrew

I'll tell you how much I love Hebrew:
Read me anything –
Genesis
Or an ad in an Israeli paper
And watch my face.
I will make half-sounds of ecstasy
And my smile will be so enormously sweet
You would think some angels were singing Psalms
Or God … was reciting to me.
I am crazy for her Holiness
And each restaurant's menu in Yerushalayim
Or Bialik poem
Gives me peace no Dante or Milton or Goethe
Could give.
I have heard Iliads of poetry,
Omar Khayyam in Farsi,
And Virgil sung as if the poet himself
Were coaching the reader.
And they move me –

But not like
The train schedule from Haifa to Tel Aviv
Or a choppy unsyntaxed note
From a student who got half the grammar I taught him
All wrong
But remembered to write
With Alefs and Zayins and Shins.
That's the way I am.
I'd rather hear the weather report
On Kol Yisrael
Than all the rhythms and music of Shakespeare."[6]

B'ahavah ("With Love"),
Dad

Discussion Questions:

- Do you believe it is important for Jews to know some Hebrew?

- Are you content to rely upon English when visiting Israel?

What a Country!

Dear Daniel and David,

I landed in Israel for the first time on June 29, 1973 when I was 23 years old. I lived there for one year, and I have returned more than 25 times. All I can say—given everything I know about Israel, its strengths and flaws, its humanity and its ills, its challenges and successes—is "What a country!"

Taking everything together, I'm amazed at the nation the Jewish people have built in the short historical span since Theodor Herzl convened the First World Zionist Congress in 1897. It is remarkable to see how many Jews have been successfully absorbed into Israeli life, raised their children and grandchildren, and renewed the Jewish people in the land that is our people's national home.

It's a singular miracle that Hebrew now flows so naturally through the lips of little children and that it's become the language of celebrated poets and literary figures.

Despite having to fight numerous wars of survival and to protect itself against terrorism and hostility from much of the world, Israel's democracy (within the Green Line) is strong and thriving, and its Declaration of Independence constantly renews the country's aspiration to be a nation that values human rights for all its citizens and inhabitants.

I'm not blind to the truth that Israel, like all democracies, is imperfect. I don't excuse the occupation of another people for a minute, as you know. But all things considered, Israel is an extraordinary success story, an experiment that has inspired hopes and dreams not just of the Jewish people, but of many peoples around the world. Even Israel's enemies esteem what it created.

The country is evolving in ways that make me proud, and I hope you'll not only bear with me but celebrate as I list some of the many reasons for the optimism I feel. Israelis generally have become gentler and kinder people over the decades; and Israel as a nation, despite the violence in its history, is a gentler and more decent place—its media image notwith-standing.

There are numerous signs that the future for Israel will be better than the past. More than 15,000 active non-governmental organizations (NGOs) in Israel—most not politically aligned—promote universal moral values, human rights, democracy, civil society, and the environment. Many small projects bring Arab Muslim Israeli citizens and Jewish Israeli citizens together to learn about one another, hear each other's stories, and develop greater compassion. Hundreds of Arab Israeli citizens and Jews, for example, travel to Auschwitz to expand their understanding and help their people comprehend the depths of historic Jewish suffering that informs our people's national narrative.

Many NGOs and groups, Jewish and Arab, aspire to do good for others. Volunteers in development towns and villages help new immigrants adjust to life in their new homes, and 150 collective communities in depressed communities seek to help impoverished children. Other programs assist Arab Israeli citizens. Muhammed Darawshe, for example, has been working with the Israeli government from his base at Givat Haviva to help educate Arab Israeli women, provide childcare while they work, and enable them to enter the workforce—thus lifting thousands of Arab Israeli citizens and families out of poverty.

A project called Yad b'Yad (Hand in Hand) is working to create a strong, inclusive, shared society in Israel. Through a network of Jewish-Arab integrated bilingual schools and organized communities, Yad b'Yad brings together thousands of Jews and Arabs in six schools and communities throughout Israel. During the "Knifing Intifada" in 2016, Arab students living in East Jerusalem stayed for weeks in the homes of their Israeli Jewish classmates because it was too difficult to get through Israeli checkpoints and come to school each morning. Arab students and Jewish students grow up together and regard each other as trusted friends despite the differences in their histories and national narratives.

Only 30 years ago there was a taboo against homosexuality in the Jewish state. Now, 150,000 people march in Tel Aviv's gay pride parade each year. There are estimated to be 750,000 LGBTQ individuals in Israel, many coming from the Orthodox world and Arab Israeli communities which shun homosexuality as deviant and against traditional religious law. The modern State of Israel accepts and welcomes them.

Israeli young people are engaged in politics in ever greater numbers—especially since the Social Justice "Cottage Cheese" rebellion of 2012 that brought 250,000 young Israelis to Rothschild Street in Tel Aviv. The young leader Stav Shafrir, a leader of that demonstration, was elected to the Knesset as a member of the Zionist Union at the age of 29, and she has made a major impact as the youngest member of the Knesset.

Schools are improving. Haredim (ultra-Orthodox) students are learning skills that can bring them into the workforce and out of poverty. Neighborhood bomb shelters, in some places, are being turned into arts centers for children.

Though racism and hostility between Arab and Jew exists, if you visit any Israeli hospital anywhere in the country, you'll see Arabs and Jews on the same wards together receiving compassionate treatment by Arab and Jewish physicians and nurses. During the Syrian civil war, badly injured Syrians were brought across the border into Israel to be treated at Israeli-operated makeshift hospitals. The same is happening in Israel just inside the Gaza border. Israel is among the leading nations working on clean environmental technologies and innovation. Israelis collect food for the increasing numbers of people in poverty.

The goodwill of Israeli Jews and Israeli Arabs in many places within Israel itself is part of the complex, hopeful reality of Israel. The extent of the good being performed every day can jolt like a drug, like electricity. It's heartening to see the generosity of spirit that pours out in so many places by so many liberal-minded Israelis who care about social justice despite the growth of extremism in the state. For example, the Reform congregation Kol Haneshama in Jerusalem supported Eritrean and Sudanese refugees. Kehilat Mevasseret Zion, a Reform synagogue community down the road from Jerusalem, worked with an absorption Center in their town to help Ethiopian Jewish immigrants adjust to Israeli life. The Reform synagogue in Modin convenes regular discussion groups between Israelis in that city and Arab Palestinian citizens of the state. There are numerous examples of this kind of Israeli Jewish activism and outreach to the "other," to strangers and the underprivileged.

Yes, there are plenty of problems facing Israel, and many are of its own making. There's shortsightedness and intolerance. There's injustice and suffering. Too many Israelis wear blinders and are oddly unaware of the injustices taking place in East Jerusalem and across the Green Line in the occupied West Bank. There's certainly far too much rage and despair and not nearly enough empathy and faith.

Israeli parents worry that the choices their government makes sentence their children to a lesser future than they would wish. Yet, at the same time they're thrilled to be raising their families in a country electric with creativity and alive with a sense of history, a place where kids can grow up with pride as Jews, filled with humanitarian impulses and a desire to help make their country a better place for everyone. Polls taken in recent years reveal that Israel ranks among the top 15 nations in the world in which its population is happy.

Our own Israeli Reform and Progressive Jewish movement is growing dramatically and attracting the engagement of 7 percent of Israeli citizens—up from 3.7 percent only eight years ago—and becoming recognized by increasing numbers of Israeli non-Orthodox Jews as a religious movement that represents their own liberal Jewish values.

Lift your eyes from the barrage of dark news and it's clear that Isaiah's vision that the Jewish people ought to be an *or lagoyim*—"a light to the nations" (42:6) is manifesting itself in a thousand rays of light.

I hope you and your peers come to appreciate this nation as I do. It is an extraordinary place.

Love,

Dad

Discussion Questions:

- After considering the positive dimensions that make the State of Israel the nation that it is, what do you believe are its greatest challenges, opportunities, and threats?

- Reflecting on your liberal American Jewish values, do you personally feel a disconnect with Israel now that you have read this book of letters to the author's children and the millennial generation?

- What are some of the points the author made that are helpful to you in thinking about the modern State of Israel in your life as a Diaspora Jew?

- Do you agree with the statement made by Rabbi Richard Hirsch that "Israel is Broadway and America is off-Broadway"?

- How do you relate to the statement of the medieval philosopher and sage Yehuda HaLevi: "My heart is in the east and the rest of me in the far reaches of the west?"

Afterword

By Daniel and David Rosove

Note: Daniel and David Rosove, Rabbi Rosove's sons, wrote their After-word in the form of a Google chat, one channel that millennials use to communicate with each other.

(davidrosove) So, Dad's book. What did you think? I loved a lot of it but I did find myself having trouble getting through some of it. I do feel a deep connection with Israel, more specifically the idea of it, but sometimes the politics and history don't break through.

(danielrosove) Some topics I identify with more than others. I have always loved Dad's narrative and perspective on Israel. It greatly influenced mine. But there are differences.

(davidrosove) Yeah, me too. What are yours?

(danielrosove) He and I share our foundational love of Israel and Zionism: a love of land and place, the Israeli people and the Hebrew language, the history and Jewish self-determination that Israel represents. He and I also agree on much of the politics.

How amazing was our first trip together as a family, right? What do you remember?

(davidrosove) You mean the one we took when I was 8 and you were 13?

(danielrosove) Yeah, in '98.

(davidrosove) Well, I remember that the first night I was so jet-lagged that my face fell directly into my pasta at that restaurant on the beach in Tel Aviv! Over 20 years later, I think to myself, "Why was I eating pasta on my first night in Israel and not hummus and pita?"

(danielrosove) Haha, right. Even before that awesome family trip, my first memories of Israel are posters at religious school of kibbutzniks working fields, and being next to Dad when he learned that Yitzhak Rabin had been shot. We were at a concert. The truth is, that's my first memory of Israeli politics and the conflict—a historic and painful introduction.

(davidrosove) Wow. I don't remember that, but I must have been with you. I was five at the time.

(danielrosove) For our generation, I think Rabin's assassination and the events that followed in the next 10-15 years—the failed peace process, the second intifada, continued violence—are anchoring events for relating to and experiencing Israel.

(davidrosove) Yeah.

(danielrosove) Think about Dad's foundational events around Israel. He was born the year Israel won the War of Independence. He grew up during the ingathering of the Jews from the ashes of the Holocaust. He was 17 during the triumph of the Six Day War and a rabbinical student in Jerusalem in '73 during the Yom Kippur War. For me, for you, and all millennials, the Israel we grew up with was one of settlements, occupation, intifada, failed peace settlements, and this iteration of the Netanyahu era. We also have Israel as the "start-up nation" and world-class generator of culture, arts, and science. Not to mention, in American politics we had 9/11, George W. Bush and the Iraq War, and then President Obama's dealings with Bibi. These are defining events in our political maturation and perspectives on Israel and American politics.

(davidrosove) I think you're right. One of my first memories of Israeli politics and the conflict was the bombing of the Sbarro pizzeria in Jerusalem. I remember it so clearly because we went to that restaurant on our first family trip.

(danielrosove) Wow, I had forgotten that.

(davidrosove) Unfortunately, our earliest memories of Israel are steeped in war and chaos, but for Dad, it was something so much different. One of the most profound parts of the book was reading Dad's description of the Maccabiah games where he and 40,000 Israelis sang Hatikvah. It actually gives me chills to imagine what it would have been like to be there. It's something that could only happen in Israel. That feeling of being a Jew is being a part of something that is so much bigger than us that inspires us.

(danielrosove) It really must have been spectacular. Those experiences stick with you.

(davidrosove) I think that even though his experience at those games is singular, that feeling of belonging to the Jewish people when in Israel, surrounded by Jews, is and should be universal. When I went on Birthright when I was 22, I tried to access that feeling of inclusion and being a Zionist, but it wasn't until we were walking down Ben Yehuda Street in Jerusalem that it finally hit me. I looked around and felt a calm go through my body when I noticed that everyone around me was Jewish. This is a feeling that you can only get in Israel, and is part of the reason why Israel is so important to me. It's a spiritual and physical home away from home for our people.

(danielrosove) I know the feelings you describe. They are singular to being in Israel. It helps me feel connected to the place, even when I feel disgusted by its politics and the conflict.

(davidrosove) It's amazing to think how Jews have been experiencing this feeling for decades, but when Dad stood for that Hatikvah, Israel was so new. It must have felt so different than it does today. It makes me wonder what it's going to be like for our kids and the next generation. Have you thought about that with Violet?

(danielrosove) Honestly, a lot. I want my daughter to feel a connection and care about Israel. As an American, she won't be in the army or pay taxes. But her elected officials, leaders, and tax dollars support Israel. America uses its political clout on the international stage to protect Israel. Israeli politics are deeply influenced by American politics and vice versa. So she needs to know that we have a stake. And she needs to know the truly extraordinary circumstances that we were born into.

(davidrosove) Absolutely.

(danielrosove) The Jewish people yearned to reestablish a Jewish state for 2,000 years. And by an accident of birth, you and I came into a world with Israel as a given. Therefore, we have the awesome responsibility to do what we can to help make it better. But I believe the greatest question before the Jewish people and our generation—just as Dad said in his book—is what do we do with Jewish power? What kind of state do we want? What is the role of the Diaspora in that project? How does Israel treat the stranger? And what can you and I do living in Los Angeles, so many thousands of miles away, to guarantee Israel's Jewish and democratic character for generations to come, all the while keeping true to our liberal and progressive values?

(davidrosove) I feel that we don't know anything else. It feels like a *given* that Israel should exist, but that feeling of it being a given can be detrimental to the longevity and security of Israel for younger generations. I don't feel the same urgency that Dad or you feel, especially since I haven't worked in Israel and Jewish politics in the U.S. like you two. What worries me is that if I am feeling this way, as someone who has been to Israel three times and feels a connection to it, what are my friends and other people my age feeling?

I know that when I talk to my friends, Israel doesn't really matter to them. Their first question always revolves around safety concerns, but otherwise, there's no mention of Jewish heritage and history or concern that the survival of our people here and around the world is linked to the survival of Israel.

(danielrosove) Totally. We were born into a world with an Israel. But just as there was no guarantee that Israel would survive its first 70 years due to threats from the outside, I believe Israel's greatest challenges now rest within. It's the continuing occupation, the settlement enterprise, and the gradual degrading of democratic institutions and beliefs. And in the Diaspora, the traditional organized American Jewish community's reluctance to counter these forces.

(davidrosove) And if those issues aren't confronted head on, I think my friends will continue to feel estranged—and their children will, too.

(danielrosove) I love how Dad spoke about the different streams of Zionism. Like him, I am a political Zionist and an aspirational Zionist. And aspirational Zionism has so much it can do and not a lot of time to do it.

(davidrosove) Do you not feel like some aspects of aspirational Zionism are a pipe dream? Like whatever utopian idea of Israel you and other people think of can never exist?

(danielrosove) I understand how it can feel that way. Dad quotes JFK: "Our problems are man-made—therefore, they can be solved by man." This undergirds all of my work in politics and social issues. I know you care deeply about the same issues, too.

(davidrosove) I know, and it does for me too. But one thing that really struck me was Dad's insistence that there needs to be forgiveness on both sides of the conflict in order for there to be peace. Although this *feels* like it's the right thing, I just cannot imagine it ever happening. It's not realistic. There's no way either side is going to forgive the other. If you think about the conflict in terms of a married couple who wants to divorce—each partner does not have to forgive the other in order for it to happen. They can still go on to live in happiness. That's kind of how I feel about Israel and the Palestinians. I think there can be a separation without having to forgive the other side.

(danielrosove) I think forgiveness and acceptance of the other's narrative and experience will likely never fully happen. And I agree that it may not need to. But the power of apology and forgiveness is extraordinary and must be a goal. Even a few generations after an eventual resolution.

(davidrosove) I agree, it has to be a goal. I just don't think it will happen any time soon.

(danielrosove) I believe, as do the vast majority of millennial American Jews, that for Israel to remain both Jewish and democratic, there must be a Palestinian state. The settlement enterprise is counter to this goal. I agree with Dad that the dominance of the ultra-Orthodox over Israeli society must be curtailed. He was right to say the only place Reform Jews are persecuted is in Israel! And the anti-democratic trends of Netanyahu and his allies will turn Israel into an illiberal democracy.

(davidrosove) It disturbs me to think about all the forces in Israel in support of these dynamics.

(danielrosove) Well, Dad beautifully said that Israel is like holding a mirror up to the Jewish people. All I can say is, we are one complicated, crazy, passionate, and amazing people! And I love being a Jew!!!

(davidrosove) Me too. I thought that was an intense line as well. And I know that there must be a Palestinian state in order for Israel to survive. I think my friends would say that, too.

(danielrosove) I got to say, one other thing really stuck out to me. Dad mentions that Israelis are united by a set of common values. This is just empirically untrue. The ultra-Orthodox don't have the same values as the secular Jews—or the vast majority of the American Jewish community for that matter. Just as the most diehard of Trump supporters do not share my values, Israeli religious and ultra-nationalist politicians and parties do not share my values. This perspective is emblematic of tension between millennial Jewish Americans and legacy/traditional Jewish establishment organizations. I know that Dad knows this but the rhetoric he used is not helpful.

(davidrosove) **Right. He spent his career building up the Reform movement in Israel precisely because the ultra-Orthodox's control of Judaism in the state doesn't meet our values.**

(danielrosove) Absolutely. For example, he references the 20,000 or so Jewish settlers who would not leave the West Bank in the event of a two-state solution. He speaks of a possible Jewish civil war or conflict. And I agree that is a real possibility.

(davidrosove) **The idea of a Jewish civil war or conflict shook me to my core. It had never occurred to me that Jews would kill other Jews.**

(danielrosove) What about Rabin?

(davidrosove) **Honestly, the more I think about it, it feels like some sort of resolution between the Palestinians and Israelis just won't happen. His book helped me understand and affirm my own love for Israel and gain a greater understanding of its complexities. Unfortunately, I feel as though I'm more pessimistic than ever that there can be some sort of resolution. The stakes are so high and each side is too stubborn to give even an inch. But do you find yourself feeling more pessimistic, as well?**

(danielrosove) With Trump and Bibi at the helm, there will be no deal. Full stop. But the fundamentals of the conflict aren't going way. Two peoples, two narratives, one piece of land. A resolution has to happen or both will go on killing each other and Israel will become less and less of a democratic Jewish home. So right now, pessimistic. But in the future, as determined as ever. It is our job to continue to engage with Israel and its people. To not turn our backs. To not give up.

(davidrosove) **I am with you. Add this to global warming, economic inequality, and more that baby boomers left for us to clean up . . . haha. But I am optimistic about us. I think we can do it.**

(danielrosove) I am too…

Appendix: The History and the Decisions that Brought Us to the Present

One thing that can make it frustrating to enter the discussion about Israel and Zionism today is that it so frequently zigs and zags back to pivotal dates and times in the last couple of centuries (not to mention millennia), which pop into the debate as shorthand for details that it's mistakenly assumed everyone knows.

It's helpful to run through some key themes and points on the timeline to show the sequence of events and evolution of thinking that brought us here. I've marked the "flash points" that are referred to again and again, as well as other key events on the timeline of Zionist and Israeli history.

The Ancient Connection to Palestine

Judaism designates four cities in ancient Israel/Palestine as holy: Jerusalem, Hebron, Tiberius, and Safed. Jews have lived in each city in small numbers for the past 2,000 years, surviving either on trading that brought them meager income, or on the goodwill of Jews living around the world who are one of Zionism's historic tethers.

The 1800s: Suffering in Russia

The Zionist movement arose in late nineteenth-century Europe, driven in part by concerns about the tenuous status of Jews in countries where anti-Semitism was strong. Political Zionism, one of Zionism's first varieties, advocated creating a Jewish state somewhere in the world that would allow Jews self-determination, independence, and freedom. It came at a time of escalating discrimination and violence against Jews, notably in Russia—home to what was then 40 percent of the world's Jewish population.

In 1791, Catherine the Great established the "Pale of Settlement" ("fenced off" region for Jews), the only area in the Russian Empire in which they were granted permanent residence. The Pale of Settlement included Belarus, Lithuania, Moldova, much of present-day Ukraine, eastern Latvia, and parts of western Russia. At its height, the Pale was home to five million Jews. Largely barred from the empire's cities, Jews of the Pale scraped by in the region's small towns called *shtetlehs*.

The late 1880s brought fierce anti-Semitic attacks on Jews living throughout the Pale. When Tsar Alexander II was assassinated, Jews were blamed. Between 1881 and 1883, anti-Jewish rioters burned homes and attacked residents in hundreds of communities.

In 1882, Alexander III enacted a series of restrictive "May Laws" aimed at discouraging Jewish mobility and freedom, including provisions that forbade new Jews from moving into areas outside towns, blocking their ability to get mortgages and leases, and limiting their ability to attend high schools and universities.

Against this backdrop, and with anti-Semitism on the rise across Europe, Jews began to flee from the Pale region in great numbers, many heading for the United States and Palestine. When attacks against Jews intensified in pogroms between 1903 and 1906, scores of women were raped and thousands of people were murdered, brutalized, and left homeless. By 1903, a major exodus from the Pale was under way.

Late 1880s and Early Twentieth Century: Political Zionism, Jewish State as Safe Space

While threats to Jews were on bold display in Russia, anti-Semitism in France emerged in 1894 when Captain Alfred Dreyfus was falsely accused of selling military secrets to Germany and then convicted of treason.

Dreyfus was Jewish and the highest-ranking Jew in the French army. A large segment of the French public presumed his guilt. The battle over the case roiled French politics, and the anti-Semitism that permeated the debate (including rallies with chants of "Death to the Jews!") shocked many, including Jewish journalist Theodor Herzl, who covered the case. Herzl (born in Budapest, Hungary) had believed Jews could assimilate in a democracy like France that advocated the individual rights of every human being. But he came away convinced that anti-Semitism was so deeply ingrained in the European psyche, so pervasive and inescapable, that the best course for Jews was to establish their own nation in which their loyalty as Jews would not be questioned and where they could be at home and be free. Herzl made the case in a highly influential 1896 small pamphlet called The State of the Jews (Der Judenstaat) and became a major voice spreading Zionist ideas throughout the Jewish world in Eastern and Western Europe and England.

As the Jews of the Pale voted with their feet to save themselves, Herzl (known as the father of "Political Zionism") pushed hard to raise political support for Jews' freedom to "live as free men on our own soil" in a state of their own. He lobbied the British, Ottomans, Roman Catholic Church, and the Russian government for support. Uganda and Argentina came up for discussion, but Palestine was the only place the European Jews would accept as their rightful national home.

1880-1903: A Wave of Migration to Israel, and the First Aliyah/First Settlement

In the early 1880s, Palestine was home to 360,000 Arabs, whose lives revolved around small villages and Bedouin shepherd culture. Another 20,000 to 25,000 Jews, two thirds of whom lived in the Old City of Jerusalem, shared the land. Jerusalem is where hundreds of Pale refugees settled starting in 1880. It is where our family stayed in the cramped Jewish quarter of the Old City until 1882—when, together with three other families, they ventured out and established Petach Tikvah (now part of metropolitan Tel Aviv) as the first Jewish settlement outside of Jerusalem or any of the other holy cities.[1]

Soon after came the first of five successive waves of migration. Each wave was called an *Aliyah* (plural, *Aliyot*—Hebrew for "going up" as in "going up to Palestine"). The First Aliyah (1881-1903) of 35,000 Jews who escaped the Russian pogroms created small cooperative farms (*moshavot*) with individual ownership and villages of independent farmers. Yemenite Jews settled south of the Old City of Jerusalem in the Arab village of Silwan, familiar today as a controversial site pitting long-time Palestinian residents against right-wing ultra-Orthodox Jews attempting to take over the neighborhood.

Late 1880s and early 1900s:

Cultural Zionism, Jewish State as Inspiring Spiritual Center

Asher Ginsberg, a Ukrainian Jewish intellectual, emphasized the importance of strengthening Jewish culture in Palestine and the Diaspora, eventually building enough support to sustain a Jewish state. He argued the central idea that reviving a Jewish national consciousness would unite Jews around the world.

Ginsberg, whose pen name was Ahad Ha-am, meaning "One of the People," was called the "Father of Cultural Zionism." He acknowledged the threat of anti-Semitism, but believed that what would ultimately serve Jews best was to create a "national spiritual center of Judaism, to which all Jews would turn with affection, and which would bind all Jews together; a center of study and learning, of language and literature, of bodily work and spiritual purification; a true miniature of the people of Israel as it ought to be...so that every Hebrew in the Diaspora will think it a privilege to behold just once 'the center of Judaism' and when he returns home will say to his friends: If you wish to see the genuine type of Jew, whether it be a Rabbi or a scholar or a writer, a farmer or an artist or a businessman – then go to Palestine and you will see it."[2]

1904-1914: The Second Aliyah, Russian Socialists, and Kibbutzim

The second wave of immigration to Palestine added 40,000 more Russian Jews. They were primarily socialists and brought with them a model of collective settlement (the kibbutz, from the Hebrew word "to bring together") in which there is no private ownership of land. David ben Gurion, who became Israel's first Prime Minister, was part of this group. Most immigrants who came in subsequent Aliyot lived on these collective settlements and in new towns and cities.

1909: Tel Aviv

Settlers established the first Hebrew city, Tel Aviv, some two decades into the migration.

1917: The Balfour Declaration

During World War I, along with horrific battles on the western European front, the British fought Germany, its allies, and the Ottoman Turks for control of the Suez Canal. The Ottomans had ruled much of the Middle East since the sixteenth century. British troops, aided by British support for an Arab uprising, took Palestine and today's Syria in what came to be known as the British Mandate. They set up a military government in Palestine and left its ally France to control Syria. Almost from the beginning, the British supported a new refuge in Palestine for Jews—believing that they would gain not only a long-term ally and a base of operations, but cut the number of Russian refugees landing in England as they diverted them to Palestine. These factors led to a historic letter from U.K. Foreign Secretary Arthur Balfour to British Zionist leader Lord Walter Rothschild, giving voice to British support for the creation of a "national home for the Jewish people" in Palestine, the first time in 2,000 years that a world power had voiced such support.

1919-1923: The Third Aliyah

This migration brought another 40,000 Eastern European Jews and coincided with the end of World War I, the establishment of the British Mandate, and the promise expressed in the Balfour Declaration. European Zionists trained these migrants in agriculture so they would be capable of establishing self-sustaining economies.

1922: A Call for Limits on Jewish Immigration to Palestine

After Arab-Jewish riots broke out in Jaffa, Great Britain approved a White Paper that called for limiting Jewish immigration based on "the economic capacity of the country to absorb new arrivals." The Zionists protested. The tide of Jewish immigration would not be stopped.

1924-1928: The Fourth Aliyah Picks Up the Pace

The Zionist goal was to bring as many Jews to live in Palestine as quickly as possible. Immigration doubled, and a new middle-class wave of Jews brought 82,000 fleeing anti-Semitism in Poland and Hungary. They moved to towns, establishing small businesses and light industry. However, many were unprepared for the harshness of life in Palestine, and 23,000 left the country for their home countries or the United States.

1929-1939: The Fifth Aliyah, a Surge Flees the Nazis

With Nazism on the rise in Germany, Jews clamored to leave Europe. In the short space of a decade, 250,000 immigrants arrived. The majority of those, 174,000, arrived from 1933—the year Hitler came to power, the Reichstag was burned and the Dachau concentration camp was completed—until 1936.

This Aliyah came mostly from Poland, Germany, Austria, Czechoslovakia, Greece, and Yemen, and included large numbers of Jewish doctors, lawyers, professors, and professionals. Musicians founded the Palestine Philharmonic Orchestra and architects introduced the famous Bauhaus architectural style (Tel Aviv has one of the largest concentrations of Bauhaus buildings in the world and is called "The White City" because of the favored Bauhaus color). By 1940, the Jewish population of Palestine hit 450,000.

1936: A Partition Plan from the British Peel Commission

With the massive Jewish migration, conflict between Arabs and Jews escalated. The British established the Peel Commission that proposed partitioning the land into an Arab state and a Jewish state. The Arabs condemned the plan while Zionist leaders were bitterly divided. According to the Israeli historian Benny Morris, Zionist leaders regarded the partition plan "as a stepping stone to some further expansion and the eventual takeover [by the Zionists] of the whole of Palestine."[3]

1936: The British Press for a Jewish
Homeland and Immigration Limits

A new British White Paper called for establishing a Jewish national home in an independent Jewish state in Palestine within 10 years. This time the British side-stepped the idea of partition. The White Paper, however, limited Jewish immigration to 75,000 for 5 years and stipulated that any further immigration would require the approval of the Arab majority population. Both the Arab and Jewish representatives rejected the plan.

1940-1945: Immigration Ceases During World War II

Astonishingly, in light of the Nazi attacks on Europe's Jews and the desperation of European Jews for a place to flee, the British allowed almost no Jews into Palestine during World War II.

The war presented a serious challenge to the Zionist leadership. On the one hand they battled against the White Paper's limits on the number of Jews allowed into the country, and on the other they fought the Nazis. Ben Gurion famously said, "We will fight with the British against Hitler as if there were no White Paper; we will fight the White Paper as if there were no war."[4]

1945-1948: The Underground Rescue Effort

After the war, the Jewish underground illegally brought in thousands of Jews from displaced persons camps. Many desperate immigrants were intercepted by British soldiers on boats and sent to Cyprus' detention camps.

In 1945, there were 200,000 Jews living in Tel Aviv. By 1948 the Jewish population in Palestine had reached 650,000.

1922-1948: The Arab Population in Palestine Doubles

By 1948, the number of Arabs living in Palestine had reached 1.2 million. Natural growth of the population was augmented by Arabs immigrating from Arabia, Transjordan, Iraq, Syria, Lebanon, and Egypt looking for work. They helped build homes, towns, and cities for the steadily arriving Jewish immigrants.

1947: U.N. Partition Plan for Palestine

The newly formed United Nations proposed a partition plan that divided Palestine into a Jewish State and an Arab State. This time, the Jews accepted the plan but the Arabs rejected it.

1947: The British Leave Palestine to the U.N.

In February 1947, the British Government, recognizing that it could not control escalating Arab-Jewish violence, announced that it would hand responsibility for Palestine to the U.N. The British withdrew its troops in June 1948.

1948: Jews Establish the State of Israel

On May 14, 1948, General Sir Alan Cunningham, the last British High Commissioner in Palestine, left Haifa to end British control over Palestine. The next day, May 15, 1948, David Ben Gurion declared the establishment of the State of Israel and became its first Prime Minister and Minister of Defense. A day later, seven Arab nations attacked Israel with the intent to destroy the infant Jewish state and "push the Jews into the sea."

This new state had a ragtag, seemingly weak army and defense force. Jews feared a second Holocaust; but when the fighting ended in armistice agreements with all the surrounding countries in 1949, Israel had expanded beyond the partition plan's proposed borders.

During the War of Independence, 6,373 Jews died defending the country against attacks by neighboring Arab nations; 10,000 Arabs died in the fighting.".

1948: Palestinian Refugee Crisis

An estimated 700,000 Palestinian Arab refugees fled the fighting in fear, or were removed by the Israeli Defense Forces (IDF) from certain areas to make Israel a more contiguous state. These Palestinian Arabs settled in refugee camps in Jordan, Lebanon, and the Gaza Strip.

1948-1951: Jews Pour into the New Jewish State

After the State of Israel was declared, anti-Semitic riots in a number of Arab countries resulted in the arrival in Israel of 700,000 Jews. In 1949-1950, Israel airlifted the entire community of 49,000 Yemenite Jews to Israel in what came to be known as "Operation Magic Carpet." These Jews had never seen an airplane before and regarded the planes as eagles carrying the Jews on their backs in an act of redemption (See Isaiah 40:31).

From 1948 to 1951, the Jewish population of Israel doubled, as 688,000 new immigrants brought the population to a total of 1,338,000 Jews. In 1949 alone, 249,954 Jewish immigrants arrived. Israel called this period of immigration *kibbutz galuyot* ("ingathering of exiles").

The new nation had to absorb these disparate newcomers—some of whom arrived with little more than the clothes on their backs—and build the state's infrastructure, educate its youth, teach newcomers Hebrew, and build the Israel Defense Forces.

1956: Israel and Allies Invade Egypt

When the President of Egypt, Gamal Abdul Nasser, nationalized and closed the Suez Canal and denied passage of ships from the Mediterranean to the east, Israel felt its commerce and security threatened. In partnership with Great Britain and France, Israel invaded Egypt. The allies' goal was to regain control of the Suez Canal and remove Nasser from power. However, pressure from the United States, the U.S.S.R. and the U.N. forced all three invading nations to withdraw.

1967: The Arab-Israeli Six-Day War

In June 1967, Israeli intelligence learned that Egypt, Syria, Lebanon, and Jordan were planning a coordinated attack on Israel to destroy the Jewish State. The Israeli government launched a pre-emptive strike to limit Jewish casualties on June 5, destroying the entire Egyptian air force as it remained on the ground. After six days of intense fighting Israel conquered Southern Lebanon, the Golan Heights, the West Bank of the Jordan River, East Jerusalem, the Old City, and the Sinai Peninsula. In less than a week of intense fighting, 776 Israeli soldiers and 18,300 Arabs died.

The world watched in stunned awe as Israel swiftly defeated an enemy that had seemed more numerous and powerful. Israelis hoped that this war would be its last and that the Arab nations would make peace with it, but that was not to be. The territory Israel occupied became the source of unending conflict.

1970s to 1990s: Israel Continues to Absorb Jewish Emigres

Some 900,000 Jews emigrated to Israel from the Soviet republics between the 1970s and the 1990s, many accompanied by non-Jewish relatives—a number that totaled an additional 300,000. A second wave of Ethiopian Jews came to Israel in a coordinated effort called Operation Solomon in 1991, creating the largest *Beta Yisrael* (House of Israel), as they are known, with a population in the world numbering 125,500.

1973: The Yom Kippur War

On the holiest day of the Jewish year, Yom Kippur, Egypt and Syria attacked Israel. The loss of Jewish life devastated Israel (2,688 Israelis and 19,000 Arabs died) and punctured the air of impenetrability that Israel's victory in the 1967 War had created. Only with a massive airlift of supplies from the United States did Israel turn the war around. Israeli troops crossed the Suez Canal, suffering heavy losses, and successfully surrounded the Egyptian army. The United States called on Israel to enter into a cease fire, thus leaving Egypt a measure of dignity. That decision bore fruit four years later.

1977: Sadat Comes to Jerusalem to Make Peace

In 1977, President Anwar Sadat of Egypt broadcast to the world that he was ready to make peace with the Jewish State. Israelis were stunned, disbelieving, and ecstatic with the possibilities Sadat's overture presented. When Sadat landed at the Lod Airport in Tel Aviv, the immediate past Israeli Prime Minister Golda Meir at that time greeted him on the red carpet and asked, "What took you so long?"

Israelis greeted Sadat as a heroic and courageous figure. Thousands lined the roads and cheered as his motorcade climbed the Judean hills toward Jerusalem, grateful that their leaders could at last sit with the leader of the largest and most powerful Arab nation, be recognized, and make peace. Israel hoped that other Arab nations would follow Egypt's example and that peace would be at hand.

President Sadat, Israel's Prime Minister Menachem Begin, and U.S. President Jimmy Carter traveled to Camp David, Maryland, to iron out a peace agreement. After grueling negotiations, Egypt and Israel signed the agreement on March 26, 1979 on the White House Lawn. Israel returned the entire Sinai Peninsula to Egypt, including two air fields and oil, and in return received the promise of peace. The sticking point in negotiations was the future of the Palestinians. The Camp David Accord promised Palestinian autonomy (shy of a state) within five years. That stipulation is still waiting to be fulfilled. However, in the nearly 40-plus years since that signing ceremony, peace with Egypt has been maintained.

1982: Lebanon War ("Operation Peace for Galilee")

Israel invaded Lebanon on June 6, 1982 after enduring repeated attacks by the Palestine Liberation Organization (PLO). When the fighting ended, Israel withdrew its troops from most of Lebanon but maintained its occupation of southern Lebanon as a buffer between the PLO and Israel. Israel remained there until Prime Minister Ehud Barak unilaterally withdrew Israeli troops in 2000. The PLO concluded that if it continued to battle Israel in the West Bank, Israel would eventually withdraw as well from there. That belief led to the First Intifada (Arabic for "rebellion") by the Palestinians in the West Bank and Gaza Strip.

1987-1991: The First Palestinian Intifada

The Intifada was a Palestinian uprising against the Israeli occupation of the West Bank and Gaza Strip. Approximately 1,200 Palestinians, 60 Israeli soldiers, and 100 Israeli civilians died in the conflict. The PLO executed 822 Palestinians accused of being Israeli collaborators.

Israel used summary arrest, detentions, beatings, shootings, house demolitions, uprooting of trees, deportations, and extended imprisonments to put down the rebellion.

The PLO demanded Israel's withdrawal from all the territories it had occupied in 1967, the lifting of curfews and removal of checkpoints. Even-

tually, the PLO called for civic non-violent resistance and the establishment of a Palestinian State in the West Bank and the Gaza Strip. For the
first time, the PLO abandoned its rhetorical demand for the "liberation
of all of Palestine" and the destruction of the State of Israel.

The Intifada gave Arafat and the PLO new confidence. A meeting
of the Palestine National Council was convened in Algiers in mid-No-
vember 1988. For the first time, the PLO recognized Israel's legitimacy,
accepted all relevant U.N. resolutions going back to November 29, 1947,
and adopted the principle of a two-state solution to the conflict.

These changes and the American victory in the Gulf War led to the
Madrid Peace Conference in 1991.

1991: The Madrid Peace Conference

Co-sponsored by the United States and the Soviet Union and attended
by Israel, the Palestinians, Jordan, Lebanon, and Syria, a series of bilateral
negotiations began between Israel and the joint Jordanian-Palestinian
delegation, Lebanon, and Syria. More bilateral meetings took place in
Washington, D.C. and Moscow.

Though the conference produced nothing concrete, the meetings inspired hope that there could be a pathway to reconciliation and peace.

1993: The Oslo Accords

On September 13, 1993, Prime Minister Yitzhak Rabin joined with
Palestinian leader Yasser Arafat and U.S. President Bill Clinton to sign
the Oslo peace accords on the White House South Lawn. These accords
promised an eventual resolution to the Israeli-Palestinian conflict. King
Hussein of Jordan and Prime Minister Yitzhak Rabin of Israel signed a
separate Israeli-Jordanian peace treaty the following year on October 26,
1994.

The Oslo process halted on November 4, 1995 when an extremist Orthodox Jewish law student assassinated Rabin as he walked to his car following a massive peace rally in Tel Aviv's Plaza of the Kings, soon to be
renamed Rabin Plaza. Rabin was murdered because right-wing religious
extremists supported by right-wing ultra-Orthodox rabbis characterized
him as a *malshin* (a "stinker" or traitor which traditional Jewish law—*hal-*

akha—deems worthy of the death penalty) and a *rodef* (a "pursuer" also deserving of death).

Rabin had just sung with hundreds of thousands of hopeful Israelis the popular peace song "Shir Lashalom" (A Song for Peace). The words were written on a piece of paper that he placed in his shirt pocket as he descended the steps to his death. Blood from his wound soaked the paper—a poignant reminder of the blood spilled in both the Jewish and Palestinian communities over the past century.

Shimon Peres, the new Israeli Prime Minister and a partner to Rabin in the Oslo peace process, attempted to continue what began at Oslo—but Palestinian terrorist attacks intensified within Israel. Israelis became polarized and cynical about Palestinian Chairman Yasser Arafat's true intentions.

2000 to the Present: Failed Attempts at Peace with the Palestinians

Israel and the Palestinians tried three more times to make peace; they failed each time. In 2000, Israel offered more than ever before, but the Palestinians refused the deal.

In 2006-2007, Israeli Prime Minister Ehud Olmert met secretly 36 times with Arafat's successor, Palestinian President Machmud Abbas; but the deal dissolved when Olmert was forced to resign after being indicted for corruption when he was the Mayor of Jerusalem.

Finally, in 2013-2014, under the leadership of American Secretary of State John Kerry, there were long and tedious negotiations between Prime Minister Netanyahu and Palestinian President Abbas—but no success.

The story is essentially a constant over the past 25 years. Israel says it wants peace but it claims that it has not had a real peace partner in the Palestinian leadership. Israel charges that the Palestinian people have not been educated to live peaceably beside Israel in a two-state solution. And many believe that despite what they say, the Palestinian leadership still wants to destroy Israel.

The Palestinians say they have accepted the existence of the State of Israel (in 1988) and want their own state. But Israel's settlement enterprise has made a contiguous Palestinian state impossible—unless dozens of small Jewish outposts and settlements are dismantled and Israeli settlers withdraw. Palestinians believe they have no real peace partner in Israel.

2000-2005: The Second Palestinian Intifada

Following the Rabin assassination and the failed Camp David negotiations in 2000, a second Intifada broke out the day after Likud Prime Ministerial Candidate Ariel Sharon made a visit to the Temple Mount in Jerusalem. Palestinians regarded the visit as a provocation and considered their subsequent violence as part of their struggle for national liberation and an end to the Israeli occupation. Israelis believe that Arafat preplanned the Intifada and used the Sharon visit as a Palestinian excuse for the violence. Many Israelis also believe that the Sharon visit was an internal power play within the Likud party.

Palestinians sent suicide bombers to restaurants, hotels, and buses to murder and terrorize Israelis. Israel used tanks, gunfire, air attacks, and targeted killings to put down the rebellion. Approximately 3,000 Palestinians, 1,000 Israelis, and 64 foreigners were killed.

2004: Israeli Withdrawal from the Gaza Strip

On February 2, 2004, Israeli Prime Minister Ariel Sharon announced his plan to transfer all Jewish settlers from the Gaza Strip back into Israel, but did so without a peace agreement. He was accused by some Israelis of rewarding terrorism. This was the second time Israel had unilaterally withdrawn from territory. The first was in Lebanon. The Palestinians regard these withdrawals as Israeli weakness and defeat.

2012: The Gaza War ("Operation Cast Lead")

Hamas took control of Gaza in a coup against the Palestinian Authority in 2007. Since the early 2000s, Hamas and other Palestinian groups in Gaza had fired 10,000 rockets indiscriminately at Israeli civilian targets from hospitals, schools, apartment buildings, and mobile launch sites. Israel launched a war to stop the rocket attacks. Though there was much destruction, Israel used pinpoint rockets to destroy Hamas facilities, rocket launch sites, homes of Hamas leaders, Hamas governing infrastructure, police training camps, and offices.

Israel charged Hamas with preventing civilians from leaving the strike zones and using them as human shields. Palestinians complained that there was no place safe to flee.

During the eventual ceasefire, Hamas continued to build hundreds of tunnels to prepare for another round of fighting against Israel. Hezbollah has done the same thing in Southern Lebanon, building tunnels and stockpiling hundreds of thousands of long-range guided missiles supplied by Iran for an eventual war against Israel. Israel has promised that if Hezbollah attacks, Israel will respond with overwhelming force.

2015-2016: The Palestinian Knife Intifada

This unique Intifada was based in grassroots Palestinian rage against Israel. Women and children took kitchen knives and attacked Israeli soldiers and civilians around the country. It was a unique Intifada in that many of the Palestinians who acted came either from East Jerusalem or inside the Green Line (the 1949 Armistice lines) and are Israeli citizens. The Intifada was not organized by the Palestinian Authority or Hamas.

Total Jewish and Arab Casualties Over a Century of Fighting

Since the 1920s, Jewish-Arab conflicts have killed 24,969 Israelis and injured 36,260; 91,105 Arabs have died and 78,038 have been injured as a result of the fighting.[5]

Notes

Letter #2 – Our American Jewish identity
and Israel—Finding Common Ground

[1] Chaim Weizmann, *Trial and Error – The Autobiography of Chaim Weizmann – First President of Israel with an Introduction by Abba Eban.* New York: Schocken, 1949, 252-253.

[2] "New Poll Shows Support Plummeting Among US Liberals, Millennials and Women," by Chemi Shalev, Haaretz, October 26, 2018.

Letter #3 – Israel and the Idea of Home

[1] "New Study of Bay Area Jews Describes Unique energetic Community," *J Weekly*, February 14, 2018. jweekly.com/2018/02/14/new-study-bay-area-jews-describes-unique-energetic-community/. The study was conducted by Steven Cohen and Jack Ukeles as commissioned by the Jewish Community Federation of San Francisco, the Peninsula, Marin, and Sonoma Counties. jta.org/2018/02/13/news-opinion/united-states/bay-area-jews-are-less-religious-and-care-less-about-israel-than-other-american-jewish-communities

[2] Bob Wofford, "In a Time of Trump, Millennial Jews Awaken to Anti-Semitism," *Politico*, October 2, 2016. politico.com/magazine/story/2016/10/donald-trump-anti-semitism-young-jews-214314

[3] "2017 Audit of Anti-Semitic Incidents - Anti-Semitic Incidents Surged Nearly 60% in 2017," *ADL Report.* February 2018. adl.org/resources/reports/2017-audit-of-anti-semitic-incidents

[4] Rabbi Donniel Hartman delivered this lecture at the Biennial Conference of the Union for Reform Judaism in Boston, MA in December 2017.

[5] In 2017, a leading public opinion research firm headed by Professor Camil Fuchs was engaged by the Israel Movement for Reform and Progressive Judaism (IMPJ) to assess the Israeli Reform movement's impact on Israeli society and how large a following of Reform Judaism currently exists in Israel. Whereas in the initial years of Israeli Reform, most of its participants were Americans who had made aliyah, Israel has never been

as open to Reform Judaism as it is today. Dr. Fuchs conducted a comprehensive survey assessing the status of the Reform Movement and religious pluralism in the State of Israel, and found: the rate of self-identification with Reform Judaism is at an historic high in Israel; more than half (56%) of the secular Israeli public say they have attended a lifecycle ceremony officiated by a Reform or Conservative rabbi, up about 10% from 2010; there is overwhelming support (81%) among the secular public for giving full equality to non-Orthodox religious streams; there is wide support (49%) among the traditional public for Reform and Conservative Judaism; a vast majority (90%) of all respondents recognized the importance of the relationship with Diaspora Jewry for the State of Israel; the number of Israelis who identify as Reform Jews has doubled since 2011 (from 3.5% to 7%). When that figure is added to the 4% of the Israeli Jewish population that identifies with Conservative Judaism, there are now nearly 800,000 Israelis (11% of the population) who identify with either Reform or Conservative Judaism in Israel. That number is equal to the number of Haredim (Ultra-Orthodox Jews) in Israel. See "URJ Releases Preliminary Findings From 2 Important Surveys Demonstrating Effectiveness Of Work In Priority Areas" — urj.org/blog/2017/11/29/urj-releases-preliminary-findings-2-important-surveys-demonstrating-effectiveness

[6] Tobias Buck, "The not-so-beautiful game of football in Israel," *Financial Times*, January 1, 2010, ft.com/content/d6849396-ef64-11de-86c4-00144feab49a

Letter #4 – Navigating between Liberalism and Zionism

[1] "Beyond Survival: Jewish Values and Aspirational Zionism," *Havruta: A Journal of Jewish Conversation*, Summer 2011, 56-63.

[2] Fyodor Dostoyevsky, *The Brothers Karamazov*. New York: Barnes and Noble Books, 2004. Book 5, Chapter 4, 227.

[3] Kurt Streeter, "Leonard Beerman Obituary," *LA Times*, December 24, 2014. latimes.com/local/obituaries/la-me-leonard-beerman-20141225-story.html

Letter #5 – Why Reform Zionism Matters

[1] Sergio Della Pergola, "World Jewish Population 2015," *American Jewish Year Book*. jewishdatabank.org/Studies/details.cfm?StudyID=803

[2] Rabbi Josh Weinberg, *Weekly ARZA Newsletter*, January 12, 2018.

Letter #6 – The International Campaign Against Israel

Note: This letter has been edited from the original article published in the *CCAR Journal: The Reform Jewish Quarterly*, Fall 2011, 90-109 and is included in *Honoring Tradition, Embracing Modernity – A Reader for the Union for Reform Judaism's Introduction to Judaism Course* (New York: CCAR Press, 2017, 526-544). It is reprinted here by permission of the CCAR.

[1] Einat Wilf, "The Intersectional Power of Zionism," *Tower Magazine*, December 15, 2016. 1thetower.org/4304-the-intersectional-power-of-zionism/

[2] UNGA Resolution 3379 was adopted on November 10, 1975 by a vote of 72 to 35 (with 32 abstentions). It "determine[d] that Zionism is a form of racism and racial discrimination."

[3] UNGA Resolution 46/86 was adopted on December 16, 1991 and revoked Resolution 3379, which had called Zionism "a form of racism." Israel demanded the revocation of Resolution 3379 as a condition of its participation in the 1991 Madrid Peace Conference. However, the damage was done as language from the original resolution was introduced into school textbooks around the world and prejudiced millions of people about Zionism and the State of Israel.

[4] Robert Rozett, "An open letter to Archbishop Desmond Tutu" by Warren Goldstein, Chief Rabbi of South Africa," *Haaretz*, September 4, 2009. https://www.haaretz.com/1.5469332

[5] Dore Gold, "Abbas? Temple Denial," *Israel Hayom Newsletter*, March 2, 2012.

[6] Jeremy Sharon, "Grand Mufti: There was never a Jewish Temple on Temple Mount," *Jerusalem Post*, October 27, 2015. jpost.com/Arab-Israeli-Conflict/Grand-mufti-There-was-never-a-Jewish-Temple-on-Temple-Mount-430131

Letter #7 – A Clash of Narratives and Rights

[1] President John F. Kennedy, *Commencement Speech at American University*, Washington, D.C., June 10, 1963. He made this statement in relationship to the threat of nuclear war and disarmament.

[2] Members of my congregation—Claudia Sobral and her writer, Sophie Sartain—produced this 40-minute documentary film. The film trailer states: *"In Israel and Palestine, the road to peace is a steep climb. For three activists, one Israeli, one Palestinian and one American, the challenges seem insurmountable. And yet they try to see and understand the humanity in 'the other' and forge connections that promote empathy, understanding and, in their wildest hopes, peace. Hotel Everest is their story."* The three peace activists include retired Israeli Colonel Eden Fuchs, Palestinian Ibrahim Issa, and Buddhist American Whit Jones.

[3] *Side by Side – Parallel Histories of Israel-Palestine*, edited by Sam Adwan, Dan Bar-On, and Eyal Naveh, New York: The New Press, 2012.

[4] Ibid., 5.

[5] "Arafat says PLO Accepted Israel," *New York Times*, December 8, 1988.

Letter #8 – Is There a Solution to the Israeli-Palestinian Conflict?

[1] See Letter #7 (A Clash of Narratives and Rights). [2] Daphna Golan-Agnon, *Jerusalem: Everyday Life in a Divided Land* (translated by Janine Woolfson), NY & London: The New Press, 2002, 13-14.

[3] Ibid.

[4] This quote by Gandhi is popularly ascribed to him, but I was not able to find the original source.

[5] Bilal Qureshi, "From Wrong To Right: A U.S. Apology For Japanese Internment," *National Public Radio – All Things Considered*, August 9, 2013. https://www.npr.org/sections/codeswitch/2013/08/09/210138278/japanese-internment-redress.

[6] Warren Throckmorton, "Apology to Native Peoples of the United States," Defense Appropriations Act of 2010 (H.R. 3326) Sec. 8113, page 435. Native American Apology Resolution 2009 – March 2, 2011. web.archive.org/web/20171213015812/www.patheos.com/blogs/warrenthrockmorton/2011/03/02/native-american-apology-resolution-2009-full-text/

[7]   *Smithsonian   Magazine.*   smithsonianmag.com/smart-news/
five-times-united-states-officially-apologized-180959254/
and report on NPR, npr.org/templates/story/story.php?storyId=93059465

[8] Yossi Alpher, *No End of Conflict – Rethinking Israel-Palestine,* New
York and London: Rowman & Littlefield, 2016.

[9] Alpher, Ibid., 76.

[10] David Pollock, 'For a State Palestinians Would Cede "Right of Return"—and More,' *Fikra Forum of the Washington Institute for Near East
Policy,* December 3, 2018. washingtoninstitute.org/fikraforum/view/for-
a-state-palestinians-would-cede-right-of-return

Letter #9 – Why Jerusalem Isn't a Unified City.

[1] When visiting Rome Jews were not to walk beneath the Arch of
Titus, a symbol of the destruction of the Second Temple in Jerusalem.

Letter #11 – Why Hebrew Matters

[1] David Hazony, "Memo to American Jews: Gulf Between Israel and
Diaspora is Growing Fast," *Jewish Forward,* April 13, 2012.
forward.com/articles/154253/memo-to-american-jews-learn-hebrew

[2]   Ahad   Ha'am,   *The Jewish State and Jewish Problem,*   1897.
jewishvirtuallibrary.org/quot-the-jewish-state-and-jewish-problem-quot-
ahad-ha-am

[3] "Zionism and the Changing Global Structure," *Jerusalem Post,* December 12, 2017. http://www.jpost.com/Opinion/Zionism-and-the-
changing-global-structure-517864

[4] David Hazony, "Israeli Identity and the Future of American Jewry,"
The Tower, June-July 2017. thetower.org/article/israeli-identity-and-the-
future-of-american-jewry/

[5] Lewis Glinert, *The Story of Hebrew,* Princeton, New Jersey:
Princeton University Press. 2017, 223, 258. Originally a letter to the
Vaad HaLashon, February 5, 1948. Accessed on August 8, 2016, at
en.hebrew-academy.org.il/wp-content/uploads/sites/2/2014/08/
dbg19481.jpg.

[6] Danny Siegel, "Hebrew," *And God Braided Eve's Hair,* New York:
United Synagogue of America, 1976, 60.

Appendix: The History and the Decisions
That Brought Us to the Present

[1] My family, the Shapiras of Petach Tikva, resented that their group of Russian immigrants to Palestine in 1880 was called the "First Aliyah." They considered themselves the "First Settlement" (Yishuv haRishon) because the term "Aliyah" had been coined by socialists as part of Ben Gurion's branding of all immigrant waves and grouping them together into the reigning philosophy of socialist Zionism. My family was not socialist.

[2] From *Summa Summarum, Nationalism and the Jewish Ethic: Basic Writings of Ahad Ha'am, New York: Schocken, 1962.*

[3] Benny Morris, Righteous Victims: A History of the Zionist-Arab Conflict, 1881-2001. New York: Vintage Books, 2001, 136-7.

[4] *David Ben-Gurion, Israel – A Personal History,* Funk & Wagnalls/ Sabra: New York & Tel Aviv, 1971, 54.

[5] Vital Statistics: Total Casualties, Arab-Israeli Conflict (1860-Present), *Jewish Virtual Library,*
jewishvirtuallibrary.org/total-casualties-arab-israeli-conflict.

Suggestions for Further Reading

Adwan, Sami, and Bar-on, Dan, and Naveh, Eyal ed., *Side by Side – Parallel Histories of Israel-Palestine*. New York: Prime (Peace Research Institute in the Middle East), 2012.

Alpher, Yossi, *No End of Conflict – Rethinking Israel-Palestine*. Lanham, Marilyn: Rowman & Littlefield, 2016.

Beinart, Peter, *The Crisis of Zionism*. New York: Times Books Henry Holt and Company, 2012.

Ben-Ami, Jeremy, *A New Voice for Israel – Fighting for the Survival of the Jewish Nation*, New York, Palgrave Macmillan, 2011.

Chabon, Michael and Waldman, Ayelet ed., *Kingdom of Olives and Ash – Writers Confront the Occupation*. New York: Harper Perennial, 2017.

Davids, Stanley M. and Englander, Lawrence A., DHL, ed. *Fragile Dialogue – New Voices of Liberal Zionism*. New York: Central Conference of American Rabbis Press, 2017.

Davids, Stanley M. and Rosove, John L., ed. *Deepening the Dialogue– American Jews and Israelis envision the Jewish-Democratic State*. New York: Central Conference of American Rabbis Press, 2019.

Eilberg, Amy, *From Enemy to Friend – Jewish Wisdom and the Pursuit of Peace*. New York: Orbis Books, 2014.

Ephron, Dan, *Killing a King – The Assassination of Yitzhak Rabin and the Remaking of Israel*. New York: W.W. Norton & Company, 2015.

Friedman, Thomas, *From Beirut to Jerusalem*. New York: Farrar Straus Giroux, 1989.

Glinert, Lewis, *The Story of Hebrew*. Princeton, New Jersey: Princeton University Press, 2017.

Golan-Agnon, Daphna, *Next Year in Jerusalem*. New York & London: The New Press, 2002.

Gold, Dore, *The Fight for Jerusalem – Radical Islam, The West, and The Future of the Holy City*. Washington, D.C.: Regency Publishing, Inc., 2007.

Halevi, Yossi Klein, *Like Dreamers – The Story of the Israeli Paratroopers Who Reunited Jerusalem and Divided a Nation*. New York: Harper Perennial, 2013.

Hertzberg, Arthur, *The Zionist Idea – A Historical Analysis and Reader*. New York: Doubleday & Company, Inc., 1959.

Hirsch, Richard G., *From the Hill to the Mount – A Reform Zionist Quest*. New York: Gefen Books, 2000.

Hirsch, Richard G., *For the Sake of Zion – Reform Zionism: a Personal Mission*. New York: URJ Press, 2011.

Kurtzer, Daniel C. ed., *Pathways to Peace – America and the Arab-Israeli Conflict*. New York: Palgrave Macmillan, 2012.

Mnookin, Robert H, *The Jewish American Paradox – Embracing Choice in a Changing World*. New York: Public Affairs, 2018.

Morris, Benny, *1948 – A History of The First Arab-Israeli War*. New Haven: Yale University Press, 2008.

Nusseibeh, Sari with David, Anthony, *Once Upon a Country – A Palestinian Life*. New York: Farrar, Straus and Giroux, 2007.

Oren, Michael B., *Six Days of War – June 1967 and the Making of the Modern Middle East*. Oxford: Oxford University Press, 2002.

Oz, Amos, *A Tale of Love and Darkness*. Orlando: Harcourt, 2002.

Rosove, John L., *Why Judaism Matters – Letters of a Liberal Rabbi to His Children and the Millennial Generation, with an Afterword by Daniel and David Rosove*. Nashville: Jewish Lights, 2017.

Shapira, Anita, *Israel – A History*. Waltham, Massachusetts: Brandeis University Press, 2012.

Shavit, Ari, *My Promised Land: The Triumph and Tragedy of Israel*. New York: Spiegel & Grau, 2013.

Tolan, Sandy, *The Lemon Tree – An Arab, A Jew, and the Heart of the Middle East*. New York: Bloomsbury, 2006.

Acknowledgements

This book represents my lifetime of love, commitment, and activism on behalf of the Jewish people and State of Israel.

Many are my friends, teachers, and mentors over five decades, and I'm grateful to them all. It's impossible to mention everyone by name, though I wish to acknowledge some.

First is Rabbi Richard Hirsch, the founding Director of the Religious Action Center of Reform Judaism in Washington, D.C., the founder of the Israel Movement for Reform and Progressive Judaism (IMPJ), the Israel Religious Action Center (IRAC), Kibbutz Yahel, and Beit Shmuel in Jerusalem.

I am grateful as well to Dick's son, Rabbi Ammiel Hirsch (Senior Rabbi of the Stephen S. Wise Free Synagogue in New York City), who first engaged me in the Association of Reform Zionists of America (ARZA). He has become the dearest of friends and is among the most articulate and thoughtful speakers about Israel and the Zionist cause in the American rabbinate.

Others include Rabbi Eric Yoffie (President Emeritus of the Union for Reform Judaism), Jeremy Ben-Ami (Founder and President of J Street), Rabbi Gilad Kariv (President and CEO of the Israel Movement for Reform and Progressive Judaism), Anat Hoffman (Executive Director of the Israel Religious Action Center and Chair of Women of the Wall), Rabbi Noa Sattath (Director of the Israel Religious Action Center), Rabbi Uri Regev (Director of Hiddush – Freedom of Religion for Israel, Inc. and founding Director of the Israel Religious Action Center), Rabbi Maya Lebovich (founding rabbi of Kehilat Mevaseret Zion), Menachem Lebovich (past director of the Himanuta division of the World Zionist Organization), Rabbi Galit Kohen-Kedem (founding Rabbi of Kehilat Kodesh v'Chol of Holon, Israel), Rabbi Meir Azari (Senior Rabbi of the Daniels Center of Tel Aviv-Yafo), Yaron Shavit (past Chair of the IMPJ and head of the ARZENU faction in the World Zionist Organization), Reuven Marko (Chair of the IMPJ), Rabbi Joshua Weinberg (Vice President for

Israel of the Union for Reform Judaism and Executive Director of the Association of Reform Zionists of America), Rabbi Leah Muehlstein (President of ARZENU, the international Reform Zionist Movement), Gusti Yehoshua Braverman (Chair of the World Zionist Organization's Department for Diaspora Activities), Rabbi Danny Freelander (President of the World Union for Progressive Judaism), Rabbi Stanley Davids (Past President of ARZA), Rabbi Rick Jacobs (President of the Union for Reform Judaism), and the officers and board who have served with me on behalf of the ARZA and ARZENU.

I am grateful to my colleagues, friends, and congregants at Temple Israel of Hollywood, and to my synagogue's board leadership that has always supported my Zionist work.

Donna Frazier Glynn, my editor, who helped me shape and hone my message on this complex and nuanced subject.

As always, I am most grateful for my wife, Barbara, who has been my partner in all things and my dearest and most cherished friend, as well as for my son Daniel and his wife Marina and my son David.